Birnbaum's
San
Francisco

MW01045515

A BIRNBAUM TRAVEL GUIDE

Alexandra Mayes Birnbaum
EDITORIAL CONSULTANT

Lois Spritzer
Editorial Director

Laura L. Brengelman
Managing Editor

Mary Callahan
Senior Editor

David Appell
Patricia Canole
Gene Gold
Jill Kadetsky
Susan McClung
Associate Editors

HarperPerennial
A Division of HarperCollinsPublishers

To Stephen, who merely made all this possible.

BIRNBAUM'S SAN FRANCISCO   . Copyright © 1995 by HarperCollins Publishers. All rights reserved. Printed in the United States of America. No part of this book may be used or reproduced in any manner whatsoever without written permission except in the case of brief quotations embodied in critical articles and reviews. For information address HarperCollins*Publishers*, 10 East 53rd Street, New York, NY 10022.

FIRST EDITION

ISSN 0749-2561 (Birnbaum Travel Guides)
ISSN 1056-4403 (San Francisco)
ISBN 0-06-278171-5 (pbk.)

95 96 97 ❖/RRD 5 4 3 2

Cover design © Drenttel Doyle Partners
Cover photograph © Jake Rajs/The Image Bank
Alamo Square, San Francisco

BIRNBAUM TRAVEL GUIDES

Bahamas, and Turks & Caicos
Berlin
Bermuda
Boston
Canada
Cancun, Cozumel & Isla Mujeres
Caribbean
Chicago
Country Inns and Back Roads
Disneyland
Eastern Europe
Europe
Europe for Business Travelers
France
Germany
Great Britain
Hawaii
Ireland
Italy
London
Los Angeles
Mexico
Miami & Ft. Lauderdale
Montreal & Quebec City
New Orleans
New York
Paris
Portugal
Rome
San Francisco
Santa Fe & Taos
South America
Spain
United States
USA for Business Travelers
Walt Disney World
Walt Disney World for Kids, By Kids
Washington, DC

Contributing Editors

David Hartley
Donna Peck
Anita Peltonen
Caryn Reading

Maps

Mark Carlson
Susan Carlson

Contents

Diversions

*A selective guide to a variety of unexpected pleasures,
pinpointing the best places to pursue them.*

Exceptional Pleasures and Treasures

Directions

Seven of the most delightful walks through San Francisco.

Foreword

It doesn't seem to matter how much of the world you visit; San Francisco still exerts a unique pull. I guess my husband, Steve Birnbaum, saw as many different cities as most folks, but when anyone asked him where he'd most like to live, "San Francisco" flowed automatically from his tongue. How can I disagree?

To begin with, San Francisco is breathtakingly beautiful. It doesn't seem to matter where you stand within the city limits, there's always a view of ocean, mountains, architecture, and/or local oddity that fills your vista. It is filling food for the soul.

The atmosphere of San Francisco—the feeling of freedom and well being—is inescapable. Everything seems possible in the City by the Bay, and while this may not really be any more likely there than elsewhere, it certainly feels as if it is.

Many folks have tried to become residents of San Francisco. But San Francisco seems to know of its unusual appeal to folks who live elsewhere, so jobs are scarce, salaries are hardly generous, and living costs are high—and then there's the summer weather . . . It is not always an easy life among the hills and between the bridges.

So absolutely the best way to see San Francisco is as a visitor, one who leaves by saying, "Boy, I wish I could live here. . . " It's the pleasure that comes from the old show business saying, "Always leave them wanting something more," and San Francisco does that better than any place I know.

We have tried to create a guide to San Francisco that's specifically organized, written, and edited for today's demanding traveler, one for whom qualitative information is infinitely more desirable than mere quantities of unappraised data. We realize that it's impossible for any single travel writer to visit thousands of restaurants (and nearly as many hotels) in any given year and provide accurate appraisals of each. And even if it were physically possible for one human being to survive such an itinerary, it would of necessity have to be done at a dead sprint, and the perceptions derived therefrom would probably be less valid than those of any other intelligent individual visiting the same establishments. It is, therefore, both impractical and undesirable (especially in a large, annually revised and updated guidebook *series* such as we offer) to have only one person provide all the data on the entire world. Instead, we have chosen what we like to describe as the "thee and me" approach to restaurant and hotel evaluation and, to a somewhat more limited degree, to the sites and sights we have included in the other sections of our text. What this really reflects is a personal sampling tempered by intelligent counsel from informed local sources.

This guidebook is directed to the "visitor," and such elements as restaurants have been specifically picked to provide the visitor with a representative, enlightening, and, above all, pleasant experience. Since so many extraneous considerations can affect the reception and service accorded a regular restaurant patron, our choices can in no way be construed as an exhaustive guide to resident dining. We think we've listed all the best places, in various price ranges, but they were chosen with a visitor's enjoyment in mind.

Other evidence of how we've tried to tailor our text to reflect modern travel habits is apparent in the section we call DIVERSIONS. Where once it was common for travelers to spend an urban visit seeing only the obvious sights, today's traveler is more likely to want to pursue a special interest or to venture off the beaten path. In response to this trend, we have collected a series of special experiences so that it is no longer necessary to wade through a pound or two of superfluous prose just to find exceptional pleasures and treasures.

Finally, I also should point out that every good travel guide is a living enterprise; that is, no part of this text is carved in stone. In our annual revisions, we refine, expand, and further hone all our material to serve your travel needs better. To this end, no contribution is of greater value to us than your personal reaction to what we have written, as well as information reflecting your own experiences while using the book. Please write to us at 10 E. 53rd St., New York, NY 10022.

We sincerely hope to hear from you.

Alexandra Mayes Birnbaum

ALEXANDRA MAYES BIRNBAUM, editorial consultant to the *Birnbaum Travel Guides*, worked with her late husband, Stephen Birnbaum, as co-editor of the series. She has been a world traveler since childhood and is known for her travel reports on radio on what's hot and what's not.

San Francisco

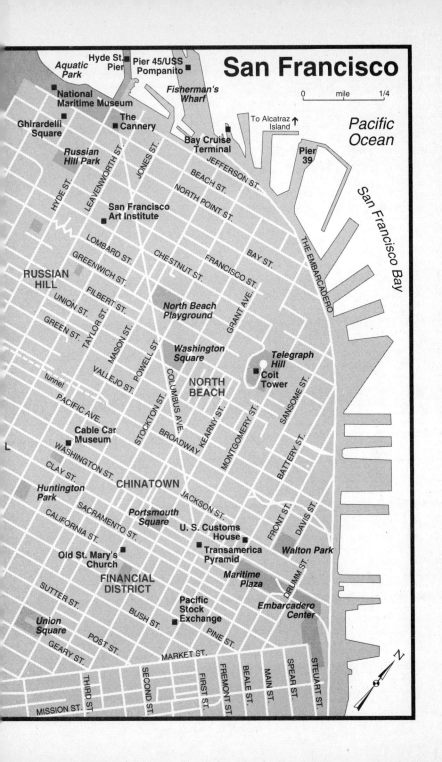

San Francisco

0   mile   1/4

Pacific Ocean

Aquatic Park

Hyde St. Pier

Pier 45/USS Pompanito

Fisherman's Wharf

National Maritime Museum

Ghirardelli Square

The Cannery

Bay Cruise Terminal

To Alcatraz Island

Pier 39

San Francisco Bay

Russian Hill Park

JEFFERSON ST.

HYDE ST.

LEAVENWORTH ST.

JONES ST.

BEACH ST.

NORTH POINT ST.

San Francisco Art Institute

THE EMBARCADERO

LOMBARD ST.

CHESTNUT ST.

FRANCISCO ST.

BAY ST.

RUSSIAN HILL

GREENWICH ST.

FILBERT ST.

UNION ST.

TAYLOR ST.

GREEN ST.

MASON ST.

POWELL ST.

GRANT AVE.

North Beach Playground

Washington Square

NORTH BEACH

Telegraph Hill

Coit Tower

SANSOME ST.

tunnel

VALLEJO ST.

PACIFIC AVE.

STOCKTON ST.

COLUMBUS AVE.

BROADWAY

KEARNY ST.

MONTGOMERY ST.

BATTERY ST.

Cable Car Museum

WASHINGTON ST.

L

CLAY ST.

CHINATOWN

JACKSON ST.

FRONT ST.

DAVIS ST.

Huntington Park

SACRAMENTO ST.

Portsmouth Square

U. S. Customs House

Walton Park

CALIFORNIA ST.

Old St. Mary's Church

Transamerica Pyramid

DRUMM ST.

Maritime Plaza

FINANCIAL DISTRICT

SUTTER ST.

BUSH ST.

Pacific Stock Exchange

Embarcadero Center

Union Square

POST ST.

PINE ST.

GEARY ST.

MARKET ST.

THIRD ST.

SECOND ST.

FIRST ST.

FREMONT ST.

BEALE ST.

MAIN ST.

SPEAR ST.

STEUART ST.

MISSION ST.

N

How to Use This Guide

A great deal of care has gone into the special organization of this guidebook, and we believe it represents a real breakthrough in the presentation of travel material.

Our text is divided into four basic sections in order to present information in the best way on every possible aspect of a vacation or business trip to San Francisco. Our aim is to highlight what's where and to provide basic information—how, when, where, how much, and what's best—to assist you in making the most intelligent choices possible.

Here is a brief summary of what you can expect to find in each section. We believe that you will find both your travel planning and en route enjoyment enhanced by having this book at your side.

GETTING READY TO GO

A mini-encyclopedia of practical travel facts with all the precise data necessary to create a successful trip to San Francisco. Here you will find how to get where you're going plus selected resources—including useful publications, and companies and organizations specializing in discount and special-interest travel—providing a wealth of information and assistance useful both before and during your trip.

THE CITY

Our report on San Francisco offers a short-stay guide, including an essay introducing the city as a historic entity and as a contemporary place to visit; an *At-a-Glance* section that's a site-by-site survey of the most important, interesting, and unique sights to see and things to do; *Sources and Resources,* a concise listing of pertinent tourism information, such as the address of the local tourist office, which sightseeing tours to take, where to find the best nightspot or hail a taxi, which shops have the finest merchandise and/or the most irresistible bargains, and where the best museums and theaters are to be found; and *Best in Town,* which lists our cost-and-quality choices of the best places to eat and sleep on a variety of budgets.

DIVERSIONS

This section is designed to help travelers find the best places in which to engage in a variety of exceptional experiences, without having to wade through endless pages of unrelated text. In every case, our particular suggestions are intended to guide you to that special place where the quality of experience is likely to be highest; this includes several areas, such as the Sonoma and Napa wine regions, that lie outside the city proper.

DIRECTIONS

Here are seven walks that cover San Francisco, and its main thoroughfares and side streets, its most spectacular landmarks, parks, neighborhoods, and vantage points.

To use this book to full advantage, take a few minutes to read the table of contents and random entries in each section to get a firsthand feel for how it all fits together. You will find that the sections of this book are building blocks designed to help you put together the best possible trip. Use them selectively as a tool, a source of ideas, a reference work for accurate facts, and a guidebook to the best buys, the most exciting sights, the most pleasant accommodations, and the tastiest foods—*the best travel experience* that you can possibly have.

Getting
Ready to Go

Getting Ready to Go

When to Go

From the standpoint of weather, there really isn't a best time to visit San Francisco. Although winter sometimes can be cool with frequent showers, for the most part, the city enjoys spring-like temperatures and sunshine in abundant supply. There also are no real off-season periods when attractions are closed.

San Francisco receives the most visitors from late spring through the summer, although conventions and other events often are scheduled in September and October. If traveling at these times, make reservations well in advance. Hotel rates can be somewhat lower from mid-November through December (sometimes through February, depending on the hotel)—except around the *Thanksgiving, Christmas,* and *New Year's* holidays.

If you have a touch-tone phone, you can call *The Weather Channel Connection* (phone: 900-WEATHER) for current weather forecasts. This service, available from *The Weather Channel* (2600 Cumberland Pkwy., Atlanta, GA 30339; phone: 404-434-6800), costs 95¢ per minute; the charge will appear on your phone bill.

Traveling by Plane

SCHEDULED FLIGHTS

Two major airports serve San Francisco: *San Francisco International Airport* and *Oakland International Airport.* Leading airlines offering flights to these airports include *Alaska Airlines, America West, American, American Eagle, Continental, Delta, Hawaiian Airlines, Midwest Express, Northwest, NW Airlink, Southwest Airlines, Tower Air, TWA, TWA Express, United, United Express, USAir,* and *USAir Express.*

FARES The great variety of airfares can be reduced to the following basic categories: first class, business class, coach (also called economy or tourist class), excursion or discount, and standby, as well as various promotional fares. For information on applicable fares and restrictions, contact the airlines listed above or ask your travel agent. Most airfares are offered for a limited time. Once you've found the lowest fare for which you can qualify, purchase your ticket as soon as possible.

RESERVATIONS Reconfirmation is not generally required on domestic flights, although it is wise to call ahead to make sure that the airline has your reservation and any special requests in its computer.

SEATING Airline seats usually are assigned on a first-come, first-served basis at check-in, although you may be able to reserve a seat when purchasing your ticket. Seating charts sometimes are available from airlines and also are included in the *Airline Seating Guide* (Carlson Publishing Co., 11132 Los Alamitos Blvd., Los Alamitos, CA 90720; phone: 310-493-4877).

SMOKING US law prohibits smoking on flights scheduled for six hours or less within the US and its territories on both domestic and international carriers. A free wallet-size guide that describes the rights of nonsmokers under current regulations is available from *ASH* (*Action on Smoking and Health;* DOT Card, 2013 H St. NW, Washington, DC 20006; phone: 202-659-4310).

SPECIAL MEALS When making your reservation, you can request one of the airline's alternate menu choices for no additional charge. Though not always required, it's a good idea to reconfirm your request the day before departure.

BAGGAGE On major airlines, passengers usually are allowed to carry on board one bag that will fit under a seat or in an overhead bin and to check two bags in the cargo hold. Specific regulations regarding dimensions and weight restrictions vary among airlines, but a checked bag usually cannot exceed 62 inches in combined dimensions (length, width, and depth), or weigh more than 70 pounds. There may be charges for additional, oversize, or overweight luggage, and for special equipment or sporting gear. Note that baggage allowances may be more limited for children (depending on the percentage of full adult fare paid). Check that the tags the airline attaches are correctly coded for your destination.

CHARTER FLIGHTS

By booking a block of seats on a specially arranged flight, charter operators frequently can offer travelers bargain airfares. If you do fly on a charter, however, read the contract's fine print carefully. Federal regulations permit charter operators to cancel a flight or assess surcharges of as much as 10% of the airfare up to 10 days before departure. You usually must book in advance, and once booked, no changes are permitted, so buy trip cancellation insurance. Also, make your check out to the company's escrow account, which provides some protection for your investment in the event that the charter operator fails. For further information, consult the publication *Jax Fax* (397 Post Rd., Darien, CT 06820; phone: 203-655-8746; fax: 203-655-6257).

DISCOUNTS ON SCHEDULED FLIGHTS

COURIER TRAVEL In return for arranging to accompany some kind of freight, a traveler pays only a portion of the total airfare (and sometimes a small registration fee). One agency that matches up would-be couriers with courier companies is *Now Voyager* (74 Varick St., Suite 307, New York, NY 10013; phone: 212-431-1616; fax: 212-334-5243).

Courier Companies

Discount Travel International (169 W. 81st St., New York, NY 10024; phone: 212-362-3636; fax: 212-362-3236; and 801 Alton Rd., Suite 1, Miami Beach, FL 33139; phone: 305-538-1616; fax: 305-673-9376).

F.B. On Board Courier Club (10225 Ryan Ave., Suite 103, Dorval, Quebec H9P 1A2, Canada; phone: 514-633-0740; fax: 514-633-0735).

Halbart Express (147-05 176th St., Jamaica, NY 11434; phone: 718-656-8279; fax: 718-244-0559).

Midnite Express (925 W. Hyde Park Blvd., Inglewood, CA 90302; phone: 310-672-1100; fax: 310-671-0107).

Way to Go Travel (6679 Sunset Blvd., Hollywood, CA 90028; phone: 213-466-1126; fax: 213-466-8994).

Publications

Insiders Guide to Air Courier Bargains, by Kelly Monaghan (The Intrepid Traveler, PO Box 438, New York, NY 10034; phone: 212-569-1081 for information; 800-356-9315 for orders; fax: 212-942-6687).

Travel Unlimited (PO Box 1058, Allston, MA 02134-1058; no phone).

CONSOLIDATORS AND BUCKET SHOPS These companies buy blocks of tickets from airlines and sell them at a discount to travel agents or directly to consumers. Since many bucket shops operate on a thin margin, be sure to check a company's record with the *Better Business Bureau*—before parting with any money.

Council Charter (205 E. 42nd St., New York, NY 10017; phone: 800-800-8222 or 212-661-0311; fax: 212-972-0194).

International Adventures (60 E. 42nd St., Room 763, New York, NY 10165; phone: 212-599-0577; fax: 212-599-3288).

Travac Tours and Charters (989 Ave. of the Americas, New York, NY 10018; phone: 800-872-8800 or 212-563-3303; fax: 212-563-3631).

Unitravel (1177 N. Warson Rd., St. Louis, MO 63132; phone: 800-325-2222 or 314-569-0900; fax: 314-569-2503).

LAST-MINUTE TRAVEL CLUBS Members of such clubs receive information on imminent trips and other bargain travel opportunities. There usually is an annual fee, although a few clubs offer free membership. Despite the names of some of the clubs listed below, you don't have to wait until literally the last minute to make travel plans.

Discount Travel International (114 Forrest Ave., Suite 203, Narberth, PA 19072; phone: 215-668-7184; fax: 215-668-9182).

FLY ASAP (PO Box 9808, Scottsdale, AZ 85252-3808; phone: 800-FLY-ASAP or 602-956-1987; fax: 602-956-6414).

Last Minute Travel (1249 Boylston St., Boston, MA 02215; phone: 800-LAST-MIN or 617-267-9800; fax: 617-424-1943).

  Moment's Notice (425 Madison Ave., New York, NY 10017; phone: 212-486-0500/1/2/3; fax: 212-486-0783).

  Spur of the Moment Cruises (411 N. Harbor Blvd., Suite 302, San Pedro, CA 90731; phone: 800-4-CRUISES or 310-521-1070 in California; 800-343-1991 elsewhere in the US; 24-hour hotline: 310-521-1060; fax: 310-521-1061).

  Traveler's Advantage (3033 S. Parker Rd., Suite 900, Aurora, CO 80014; phone: 800-548-1116 or 800-835-8747; fax: 303-368-3985).

  Vacations to Go (1502 Augusta Dr., Suite 415, Houston, TX 77057; phone: 713-974-2121 in Texas; 800-338-4962 elsewhere in the US; fax: 713-974-0445).

  Worldwide Discount Travel Club (1674 Meridian Ave., Miami Beach, FL 33139; phone: 305-534-2082; fax: 305-534-2070).

GENERIC AIR TRAVEL These organizations operate much like an ordinary airline standby service, except that they offer seats on not one but several scheduled and charter airlines. One pioneer of generic flights is *Airhitch* (2790 Broadway, Suite 100, New York, NY 10025; phone: 212-864-2000).

BARTERED TRAVEL SOURCES Barter—the exchange of commodities or services in lieu of cash payment—is a common practice among travel suppliers. Companies that have obtained travel services through barter may sell these services at substantial discounts to travel clubs, who pass along the savings to members. One organization offering bartered travel opportunities is *Travel World Leisure Club* (225 W. 34th St., Suite 909, New York, NY 10122; phone: 800-444-TWLC or 212-239-4855; fax: 212-564-5158).

CONSUMER PROTECTION

Passengers whose complaints have not been satisfactorily addressed by the airline can contact the *US Department of Transportation* (*DOT;* Consumer Affairs Division, 400 Seventh St. SW, Room 10405, Washington, DC 20590; phone: 202-366-2220). Also see *Fly Rights* (Publication #050-000-00513-5; *US Government Printing Office,* PO Box 371954, Pittsburgh, PA 15250-7954; phone: 202-783-3238; fax: 202-512-2250). If you have safety-related questions or concerns, write to the *Federal Aviation Administration* (*FAA;* 800 Independence Ave. SW, Washington, DC 20591) or call the *FAA Consumer Hotline* (phone: 800-322-7873).

On Arrival

FROM THE AIRPORTS TO THE CITY

San Francisco International Airport is 16 miles and about a 30-minute drive from the city center—if it's not rush hour. Taxi fare from the airport to downtown ranges from $25 to $30. *SFO Airporter* (phone: 415-495-8404) buses link the airport and downtown hotels and cost $8 one way and $14 round trip. *SamTrans* buses (phone: 800-660-4287 in the San Francisco Bay Area; 415-508-6200 elsewhere in the US; fax: 415-508-6443) serve both the peninsula and downtown; the fare ranges from 85¢ to $1.75. Various shuttle services also connect the airport to city and suburban locations (costs vary); for schedules and other information, call the airport information line (phone: 800-SFO-2008 or 415-876-7809 in San Francisco; 800-435-9736 elsewhere in the US).

Oakland International Airport is about 35 miles from San Francisco—about a 45-minute drive from the financial district during non-rush hours. Cab fare should run between $45 and $50. Shuttles also operate between this airport and San Francisco and Oakland. Rail service is available via the *Bay Area Rapid Transit* system (*BART;* Attn.: Customer Service, 800 Madison St., Oakland, CA 94607; phone: 510-464-6000; fax: 510-464-6247); from the airport, take a shuttle bus to the *Oakland Coliseum Arena* ($2), and then take a *BART* train to Montgomery Street in downtown San Francisco ($1.90).

RENTING A CAR

You can rent a car through a travel agent or national rental firm before leaving home, or from a local company once in San Francisco. Reserve in advance. If you do drive in San Francisco, remember that cable cars and pedestrians always have the right of way. Also, be sure to curb your wheels when parking on one of the city's steep hills.

Most car rental companies require a credit card, although some will accept a substantial cash deposit. The minimum age to rent a car is set by the company; some also may impose special conditions on drivers above a certain age. Electing to pay for collision damage waiver (CDW) protection will add to the cost of renting a car, but releases you from financial liability for the vehicle. Additional costs include drop-off charges or one-way service fees.

Car Rental Companies

Ace Rent-A-Car (phone: 415-771-7711).
Agency Rent-A-Car (phone: 800-321-1972).
Alamo (phone: 800-327-9633).
Avis (phone: 800-331-1212).
Bay Area Rentals (phone: 415-621-8989 or 415-441-4779).
Bob Leech Auto Rental (phone: 800-325-1240, 415-583-2727, or 415-583-4453).
Budget (phone: 800-527-0700).
Discount Rent-A-Car (phone: 415-928-4659).
Dollar Rent A Car (phone: 800-800-4000).
Enterprise Rent-A-Car (phone: 800-325-8007).
Flat Rate Rent-A-Car (phone: 800-433-3058 or 415-583-9232).
Hertz (phone: 800-654-3131).

Lloyd's International Rent-A-Car: (phone: 800-654-7037).
National (phone: 800-CAR-RENT).
Payless (phone: 800-PAYLESS).
Sears (phone: 800-527-0770).
Snappy Car Rental (phone: 800-669-4802).
Thrifty (phone: 800-367-2277).

NOTE

Rent-A-Wreck (phone: 415-851-2627) rents cars that are well worn but (presumably) mechanically sound. *Sunbelt Car Rental* (phone: 415-771-9191 or 415-692-6640) rents sports cars and luxury models.

Package Tours

A package is a collection of travel services that can be purchased in a single transaction. Its principal advantages are convenience and economy—the cost usually is lower than that of the same services purchased separately. Tour programs generally can be divided into two categories: escorted or locally hosted (with a set itinerary), and independent (usually more flexible).

When considering a package tour, read the brochure *carefully* to determine exactly what is included and any conditions that may apply, and check the company's record with the *Better Business Bureau.* The *United States Tour Operators Association* (*USTOA;* 211 E. 51st St., Suite 12B, New York, NY 10022; phone: 212-750-7371; fax: 212-421-1285) also can be helpful in determining a package tour operator's reliability. As with charter flights, to safeguard your funds, always make your check out to the company's escrow account.

Many tour operators offer packages focused on special interests such as the arts, local history, sports, and other recreations. *All Adventure Travel* (5589 Arapahoe St., Suite 208, Boulder, CO 80303; phone: 800-537-4025 or 303-440-7924; fax: 303-440-4160) represents such specialized packagers. Many also are listed in the *Specialty Travel Index* (305 San Anselmo Ave., Suite 313, San Anselmo, CA 94960; phone: 415-459-4900 in California; 800-442-4922 elsewhere in the US; fax: 415-459-4974). A number of companies offer half- or full-day sightseeing tours of the city, as well as excursions to nearby attractions, such as the wine country, Monterey, and Carmel.

Package Tour Operators

Adventure Tours (10612 Beaver Dam Rd., Hunt Valley, MD 21030-2205; phone: 410-785-3500 in Baltimore; 800-638-9040 elsewhere in the US; fax: 410-584-2271).
Alaska Airlines Vacations (PO Box 68900, Seattle, WA; phone: 800-468-2248; fax: 206-433-3374).

American Airlines FlyAAway Vacations (offices throughout the US; phone: 800-321-2121).

Backroads (1516 Fifth St., Berkeley, CA 94710-1740; phone: 800-462-2848 or 510-527-1555; fax: 510-527-1444).

Butterfield & Robinson (70 Bond St., Suite 300, Toronto, Ontario M5B 1X3, Canada; phone: 800-387-1147 or 416-864-1354; fax: 416-864-0541).

Certified Vacations (110 E. Broward Blvd., Ft. Lauderdale, FL 33302; phone: 800-233-7260 or 305-522-1440; fax: 305-357-4687).

Classic America (1 N. First St., San Jose, CA 95113; phone: 800-221-3949 or 408-287-4550; fax: 408-287-9272).

Collette Tours (162 Middle St., Pawtucket, RI 02860; phone: 800-752-2655 in New England; 800-832-4656 elsewhere in the US; fax: 401-727-4745).

Continental Grand Destinations (offices throughout the US; phone: 800-634-5555).

Dailey-Thorp (330 W. 58th St., New York, NY 10019-1817; phone: 212-307-1555; fax: 212-974-1420).

Dan Dipert Tours (PO Box 580, Arlington, TX 76004-0580; phone: 800-433-5335 or 817-543-3710; fax: 817-543-3729).

Delta's Dream Vacations (PO Box 1525, Ft. Lauderdale, FL 33302; phone: 800-872-7786).

Domenico Tours (751 Broadway, Bayonne, NJ 07002; phone: 800-554-8687, 201-823-8687, or 212-757-8687; fax: 201-823-1527).

Funway Holidays Funjet (PO Box 1460, Milwaukee, WI 53201-1460; phone: 800-558-3050 for reservations; 800-558-3060 for customer service).

Globetrotters SuperCities (139 Main St., Cambridge, MA 02142; phone: 800-333-1234 or 617-621-0099; fax: 617-577-8380).

Globus/Cosmos (5301 S. Federal Circle, Littleton, CO 80123; phone: 800-221-0090, 800-556-5454, or 303-797-2800; fax: 303-347-2080).

GOGO Tours (69 Spring St., Ramsey, NJ 07446-0507; phone: 201-934-3759).

Jefferson Tours (1206 Currie Ave., Minneapolis, MN 55403; phone: 800-767-7433 or 612-338-4174; fax: 612-332-5532).

Kerrville Tours (PO Box 79, Shreveport, LA 71161-0079; phone: 800-442-8705 or 318-227-2882; fax: 318-227-2486).

Le Ob's Tours (4635 Touro St., New Orleans, LA 70122-3933; phone: 504-288-3478; fax: 504-288-8517).

Marathon Tours (108 Main St., Charlestown, MA 02129; phone: 800-444-4097 or 617-242-7845; fax: 617-242-7686).

Maupintour (PO Box 807, Lawrence, KS 66044; phone: 800-255-4266 or 913-843-1211; fax: 913-843-8351).

Mayflower (1225 Warren Ave., Downers Grove, IL 60515; phone: 800-323-7604 or 708-960-3430; fax: 708-960-3575).

MLT Vacations and Northwest World Vacations (*MLT*, 5130 Hwy. 101, Minnetonka, MN 55345; phone: 800-328-0025 or 612-989-5000; fax: 612-474-0725).

New England Vacation Tours (PO Box 560, West Dover, VT 05356; phone: 800-742-7669 or 802-464-2076; fax: 802-464-2629).

Saga International Holidays (222 Berkeley St., Boston, MA 02116; phone: 800-343-0273 or 617-262-2262).

Sunmakers (15375 SE 30th Pl., Suite 350, Bellevue, WA 98007; phone: 800-841-4321 or 206-643-8180; fax: 800-323-2231).

Tours and Travel Odyssey (230 E. McClellan Ave., Livingston, NJ 07039; phone: 800-527-2989 or 201-992-5459; fax: 201-994-1618).

TravelTours International (250 W. 49th St., Suite 600, New York, NY 10019; phone: 800-767-8777 or 212-262-0700; fax: 212-944-5854).

Trek America (PO Box 470, Blairstown, NJ 07825; phone: 800-221-0596 or 908-362-9198; fax: 908-362-9313).

TWA Getaway Vacations (Getaway Vacation Center, 10 E. Stow Rd., Marlton, NJ 08053; phone: 800-GETAWAY; fax: 609-985-4125).

United Airlines Vacations (PO Box 24580, Milwaukee, WI 53224-0580; phone: 800-328-6877).

Companies Offering Day Tours

Blue & Gold Fleet (Pier 39, Box Z-2, San Francisco, CA 94133-1011; phone: 415-705-5555; 415-705-5444 for recorded information; fax: 415-392-3610).

Cable Car Charters (2830 Geary Blvd., San Francisco, CA 94118; phone: 800-562-7383 or 415-922-2425; fax: 415-922-1336).

Chinatown Discovery Tours (812 Clay St., San Francisco, CA 94108; phone: 415-982-8839; fax: 415-397-2120).

Cruisin' the Castro from an Historical Perspective (375 Lexington St., San Francisco, CA 94110; phone: 415-550-8110).

Golden Gate Tours and Convention Services (870 Market St., Suite 782, San Francisco, CA 94102; phone: 415-788-5775).

Gray Line Tours of San Francisco (350 Eighth St., San Francisco, CA 94103; phone: 800-826-0202 or 415-558-9400 in San Francisco; 800-99-GRAY-LINE elsewhere in the US; fax: 415-554-0349).

Great Pacific Tour Company (518 Octavia St., San Francisco, CA 94102; phone: 415-626-4499; fax: 415-626-7073).

Helen's Walk Tour (PO Box 9164, Berkeley, CA 94709; phone: 510-524-4544).

Quality Tours (5003 Palmetto Ave., Suite 83, Pacifica, CA 94044; phone: 415-994-5054).

Red & White Fleet (Pier 41, Fisherman's Wharf, San Francisco, CA 94133; phone: 800-BAY-CRUISE, 415-546-BOAT, or 415-546-2700; fax: 415-546-2623).

> *San Francisco Helicopter Tours* (PO Box 4115, Oakland, CA 94614; phone: 800-400-2404 or 510-635-4500; fax: 510-769-0520).
>
> *Tower Tours* (77 Jefferson St., San Francisco, CA 94133; phone: 415-434-8687; fax: 415-781-8687).
>
> *Wok Wiz Chinatown Walking Tours* (750 Kearny St., Suite 800, San Francisco, CA 94044; phone: 415-355-9657; fax: 415-355-5928).

Insurance

The first person with whom you should discuss travel insurance is your own insurance broker. You may discover that the insurance you already carry protects you adequately while traveling and that you need little additional coverage. If you charge travel services, the credit card company also may provide some insurance coverage (and other safeguards).

Types of Travel Insurance

Automobile insurance: Provides collision, theft, property damage, and personal liability protection while driving.

Baggage and personal effects insurance: Protects your bags and their contents in case of damage or theft at any point during your travels.

Default and/or bankruptcy insurance: Provides coverage in the event of default and/or bankruptcy on the part of the tour operator, airline, or other travel supplier.

Flight insurance: Covers accidental injury or death while flying.

Personal accident and sickness insurance: Covers cases of illness, injury, or death in an accident while traveling.

Trip cancellation and interruption insurance: Guarantees a refund if you must cancel a trip; may reimburse you for additional travel costs incurred in catching up with a tour or traveling home early.

Combination policies: Include any or all of the above.

Disabled Travelers

Make travel arrangements well in advance. Specify to all services involved the nature of your disability to determine if there are accommodations and facilities that meet your needs. For detailed information on accessibility in San Francisco, contact the *Mayor's Disability Coordinator* (10 United Nations Plaza, Suite 600, San Francisco, CA 94102; phone: 415-554-8925; TDD: 415-554-8749; fax: 415-564-8769). Accessibility information for public transportation is available from *Bay Area Rapid Transit* (*BART;* 800 Madison St., Oakland, CA 94607; phone: 510-404-6000; TDD: 510-839-2238; fax: 510-464-6247) and the *San Francisco Municipal Railway* (949 Presidio Ave., San Francisco, CA 94115; phone: 415-923-6142 or 415-673-MUNI; fax: 415-923-6166).

Organizations

ACCENT on Living (PO Box 700, Bloomington, IL 61702; phone: 800-787-8444 or 309-378-2961; fax: 309-378-4420).

Access: The Foundation for Accessibility by the Disabled (PO Box 356, Malverne, NY 11565; phone/fax: 516-887-5798).

American Foundation for the Blind (15 W. 16th St., New York, NY 10011; phone: 800-232-5463 or 212-620-2147; fax: 212-727-7418).

Information Center for Individuals with Disabilities (Ft. Point Pl., 27-43 Wormwood St., Boston, MA 02210; phone: 800-462-5015 in Massachusetts; 617-727-5540 elsewhere in the US; TDD: 617-345-9743; fax: 617-345-5318).

Mobility International (main office: 228 Borough High St., London SE1 1JX, England; phone: 44-171-403-5688; fax: 44-171-378-1292; US office: *MIUSA,* PO Box 10767, Eugene, OR 97440; phone/TDD: 503-343-1284; fax: 503-343-6812).

Moss Rehabilitation Hospital Travel Information Service (telephone referrals only; phone: 215-456-9600; TDD: 215-456-9602).

National Rehabilitation Information Center (8455 Colesville Rd., Suite 935, Silver Spring, MD 20910; phone: 301-588-9284; fax: 301-587-1967).

Paralyzed Veterans of America (*PVA;* PVA/ATTS Program, 801 18th St. NW, Washington, DC 20006; phone: 202-872-1300 in Washington, DC; 800-424-8200 elsewhere in the US; fax: 202-785-4452).

Royal Association for Disability and Rehabilitation (*RADAR;* 12 City Forum, 250 City Rd., London EC1V 8AF, England; phone: 44-171-250-3222; fax: 44-171-250-0212).

Society for the Advancement of Travel for the Handicapped (*SATH;* 347 Fifth Ave., Suite 610, New York, NY 10016; phone: 212-447-7284; fax: 212-725-8253).

Travel Industry and Disabled Exchange (*TIDE;* 5435 Donna Ave., Tarzana, CA 91356; phone: 818-368-5648).

Publications

Access Travel: A Guide to the Accessibility of Airport Terminals (Consumer Information Center, Dept. 578Z, Pueblo, CO 81009; phone: 719-948-3334).

Air Transportation of Handicapped Persons (Publication #AC-120-32; *US Department of Transportation,* Distribution Unit, Publications Section, M-443-2, 400 Seventh St. SW, Washington, DC 20590; phone: 202-366-0039).

The Diabetic Traveler (PO Box 8223 RW, Stamford, CT 06905; phone: 203-327-5832; fax: 203-975-1748).

Directory of Travel Agencies for the Disabled and Travel for the Disabled, both by Helen Hecker (Twin Peaks Press, PO Box 129, Vancouver,

WA 98666; phone: 800-637-CALM or 206-694-2462; fax: 206-696-3210).

Guide to Traveling with Arthritis (Upjohn Company, PO Box 989, Dearborn, MI 48121; phone: 800-253-9860).

The Handicapped Driver's Mobility Guide (*American Automobile Association,* 1000 AAA Dr., Heathrow, FL 32746-5080; phone: 407-444-7000; fax: 407-444-7380).

Handicapped Travel Newsletter (PO Box 269, Athens, TX 75751; phone/fax: 903-677-1260).

Handi-Travel: A Resource Book for Disabled and Elderly Travellers, by Cinnie Noble (*Canadian Rehabilitation Council for the Disabled,* 45 Sheppard Ave. E., Suite 801, Toronto, Ontario M2N 5W9, Canada; phone/TDD: 416-250-7490; fax: 416-229-1371).

Incapacitated Passengers Air Travel Guide (*International Air Transport Association,* Publications Sales Department, 2000 Peel St., Montreal, Quebec H3A 2R4, Canada; phone: 514-844-6311; fax: 514-844-5286).

Ticket to Safe Travel (*American Diabetes Association,* 1660 Duke St., Alexandria, VA 22314; phone: 800-232-3472 or 703-549-1500; fax: 703-836-7439).

Travel for the Patient with Chronic Obstructive Pulmonary Disease (Dr. Harold Silver, 1601 18th St. NW, Washington, DC 20009; phone: 202-667-0134; fax: 202-667-0148).

Travel Tips for Hearing-Impaired People (*American Academy of Otolaryngology,* 1 Prince St., Alexandria, VA 22314; phone: 703-836-4444; fax: 703-683-5100).

Travel Tips for People with Arthritis (*Arthritis Foundation,* 1314 Spring St. NW, Atlanta, GA 30309; phone: 800-283-7800 or 404-872-7100; fax: 404-872-0457).

Traveling Like Everybody Else: A Practical Guide for Disabled Travelers, by Jacqueline Freedman and Susan Gersten (Modan Publishing, PO Box 1202, Bellmore, NY 11710; phone: 516-679-1380; fax 516-679-1448).

The Wheelchair Traveler, by Douglass R. Annand (123 Ball Hill Rd., Milford, NH 03055; phone: 603-673-4539).

Package Tour Operators

Accessible Journeys (35 W. Sellers Ave., Ridley Park, PA 19078; phone: 800-846-4537 or 215-521-0339; fax: 215-521-6959).

Accessible Tours/Directions Unlimited (Attn.: Lois Bonnani, 720 N. Bedford Rd., Bedford Hills, NY 10507; phone: 800-533-5343 or 914-241-1700; fax: 914-241-0243).

Beehive Business and Leisure Travel (1130 W. Center St., N. Salt Lake, UT 84054; phone: 800-777-5727 or 801-292-4445; fax: 801-298-9460).

Classic Travel Service (8 W. 40th St., New York, NY 10018; phone: 212-869-2560 in New York State; 800-247-0909 elsewhere in the US; fax: 212-944-4493).

Evergreen Travel Service (4114 198th St. SW, Suite 13, Lynnwood, WA 98036-6742; phone: 800-435-2288 or 206-776-1184; fax: 206-775-0728).

Flying Wheels Travel (143 W. Bridge St., PO Box 382, Owatonna, MN 55060; phone: 800-535-6790 or 507-451-5005; fax: 507-451-1685).

Good Neighbor Travel Service (124 S. Main St., Viroqua, WI 54665; phone: 800-338-3245 or 608-637-2128; fax: 608-637-3030).

The Guided Tour (7900 Old York Rd., Suite 114B, Elkins Park, PA 19117-2339; phone: 800-783-5841 or 215-782-1370; fax: 215-635-2637).

Hinsdale Travel (201 E. Ogden Ave., Hinsdale, IL 60521; phone: 708-325-1335 or 708-469-7349; fax: 708-325-1342).

MedEscort International (*ABE International Airport,* PO Box 8766, Allentown, PA 18105-8766; phone: 800-255-7182 or 215-791-3111; fax: 215-791-9189).

Prestige World Travel (5710-X High Point Rd., Greensboro, NC 27407; phone: 800-476-7737 or 910-292-6690; fax: 910-632-9404).

Sprout (893 Amsterdam Ave., New York, NY 10025; phone: 212-222-9575; fax: 212-222-9768).

Weston Travel Agency (134 N. Cass Ave., Westmont, IL 60559; phone: 708-968-2513 in Illinois; 800-633-3725 elsewhere in the US; fax: 708-968-2539).

SPECIAL SERVICES

Wheelchair Getaways (733 N. Van Ness, Fresno, CA 93728; phone: 800-638-1972, 800-638-1912, or 209-441-7577; fax: 209-261-2604) rents vans designed to accommodate wheelchairs.

Single Travelers

The travel industry is not very fair to people who vacation by themselves—they often end up paying more than those traveling in pairs. There are services catering to single travelers, however, that match travel companions, offer travel arrangements with shared accommodations, and provide information and discounts. Useful publications include *Going Solo* (Doerfer Communications, PO Box 123, Apalachicola, FL 32329; phone/fax: 904-653-8848) and *Traveling on Your Own,* by Eleanor Berman (Random House, Order Dept., 400 Hahn Rd., Westminster, MD 21157; phone: 800-733-3000; fax: 800-659-2436).

Organizations and Companies

Contiki Holidays (300 Plaza Alicante, Suite 900, Garden Grove, CA 92640; phone: 800-466-0610 or 714-740-0808; fax: 714-740-0818).

Gallivanting (515 E. 79th St., Suite 20F, New York, NY 10021; phone: 800-933-9699 or 212-988-0617; fax: 212-988-0144).

Globus/Cosmos (5301 S. Federal Circle, Littleton, CO 80123; phone: 800-221-0090, 800-556-5454, or 303-797-2800; fax: 303-347-2080).

Jane's International and Sophisticated Women Travelers (2603 Bath Ave., Brooklyn, NY 11214; phone: 718-266-2045; fax: 718-266-4062).

Marion Smith Singles (611 Prescott Pl., N. Woodmere, NY 11581; phone: 516-791-4852, 516-791-4865, or 212-944-2112; fax: 516-791-4879).

Partners-in-Travel (11660 Chenault St., Suite 119, Los Angeles, CA 90049; phone: 310-476-4869).

Singles in Motion (545 W. 236th St., Riverdale, NY 10463; phone/fax: 718-884-4464).

Singleworld (401 Theodore Fremd Ave., Rye, NY 10580; phone: 800-223-6490 or 914-967-3334; fax: 914-967-7395).

Solo Flights (63 High Noon Rd., Weston, CT 06883; phone: 800-266-1566 or 203-226-9993).

Suddenly Singles Tours (161 Dreiser Loop, Bronx, NY 10475; phone: 718-379-8800 in New York City; 800-859-8396 elsewhere in the US; fax: 718-379-8858).

Travel Companion Exchange (PO Box 833, Amityville, NY 11701; phone: 516-454-0880; fax: 516-454-0170).

Travel Companions (Atrium Financial Center, 1515 N. Federal Hwy., Suite 300, Boca Raton, FL 33432; phone: 800-383-7211 or 407-393-6448; fax: 407-451-8560).

Travel in Two's (239 N. Broadway, Suite 3, N. Tarrytown, NY 10591; phone: 914-631-8301 in New York State; 800-692-5252 elsewhere in the US).

Umbrella Singles (PO Box 157, Woodbourne, NY 12788; phone: 800-537-2797 or 914-434-6871; fax: 914-434-3532).

Older Travelers

Special discounts and more free time are just two factors that have given older travelers a chance to see the world at affordable prices. Many travel suppliers offer senior discounts—sometimes only to members of certain senior citizens organizations (which provide benefits of their own). When considering a particular package, make sure the facilities—and the pace of the tour—match your needs and physical condition.

Publications

The Mature Traveler (PO Box 50820, Reno, NV 89513-0820; phone: 702-786-7419).

The Senior Citizen's Guide to Budget Travel in the US and Canada, by Paige Palmer (Pilot Books, 103 Cooper St., Babylon, NY 11702; phone: 516-422-2225; fax: 516-422-2227).

Take a Camel to Lunch and Other Adventures for Mature Travelers, by Nancy O'Connell (Bristol Publishing Enterprises, PO Box 1737, San Leandro, CA 94577; phone: 510-895-4461 in California; 800-346-4889 elsewhere in the US; fax: 510-895-4459).

Unbelievably Good Deals & Great Adventures That You Absolutely Can't Get Unless You're Over 50, by Joan Rattner Heilman (Contemporary Books, 1200 Stetson Ave., Chicago, IL 60601; phone: 312-782-9181; fax: 312-540-4687).

Organizations

American Association of Retired Persons (*AARP;* 601 E St. NW, Washington, DC 20049; phone: 202-434-2277).

Golden Companions (PO Box 754, Pullman, WA 99163-0754; phone: 208-858-2183).

Mature Outlook (Customer Service Center, 6001 N. Clark St., Chicago, IL 60660; phone: 800-336-6330).

National Council of Senior Citizens (1331 F St. NW, Washington, DC 20004; phone: 202-347-8800; fax: 202-624-9595).

Package Tour Operators

Elderhostel (75 Federal St., Boston, MA 02110-1941; phone: 617-426-7788; fax: 617-426-8351).

Evergreen Travel Service (4114 198th St. SW, Suite 13, Lynnwood, WA 98036-6742; phone: 800-435-2288 or 206-776-1184; fax: 206-775-0728).

Gadabout Tours (700 E. Tahquitz Canyon Way, Palm Springs, CA 92262; phone: 800-952-5068 or 619-325-5556; fax: 619-325-5127).

Grand Circle Travel (347 Congress St., Boston, MA 02210; phone: 800-221-2610 or 617-350-7500; fax: 617-423-0445).

Grandtravel (6900 Wisconsin Ave., Suite 706, Chevy Chase, MD 20815; phone: 800-247-7651 or 301-986-0790; fax: 301-913-0166).

Interhostel (*University of New Hampshire,* Division of Continuing Education, 6 Garrison Ave., Durham, NH 03824; phone: 800-733-9753 or 603-862-1147; fax: 603-862-1113).

Mature Tours (c/o *Solo Flights,* 63 High Noon Rd., Weston, CT 06883; phone: 800-266-1566 or 203-226-9993).

OmniTours (104 Wilmot Rd., Deerfield, IL 60015; phone: 800-962-0060 or 708-374-0088; fax: 708-374-9515).

Saga International Holidays (222 Berkeley St., Boston, MA 02116; phone: 800-343-0273 or 617-262-2262; fax: 617-375-5950).

Money Matters

CREDIT CARDS AND TRAVELER'S CHECKS

Most major credit cards enjoy wide domestic and international acceptance; however, not every hotel, restaurant, or shop in San Francisco accepts all (or in some cases any) credit cards. It's also wise to carry traveler's checks while on the road, since they are widely accepted and replaceable if stolen or lost. You can buy traveler's checks at banks and some are available by mail or phone. Keep a separate list of all traveler's checks (noting those that you have cashed) and the names and numbers of your credit cards. Both traveler's check and credit card companies have international numbers to call for information or in the event of loss or theft.

CASH MACHINES

Automated teller machines (ATMs) are increasingly common worldwide, and most banks participate in international ATM networks such as *CIRRUS* (phone: 800-4-CIRRUS) and *PLUS* (phone: 800-THE-PLUS). Cardholders can withdraw cash from any machine in the same network using either a "bank" card or, in some cases, a credit card. Additional information on ATMs and networks can be obtained from your bank or credit card company.

SENDING MONEY

Should the need arise, you can have money sent to you in San Francisco via the services provided by *American Express MoneyGram* (phone: 800-926-9400 for information; 800-866-8800 for money transfers) or *Western Union Financial Services* (phone: 800-325-6000 or 800-325-4176).

Time Zone

San Francisco is in the pacific standard time zone. Daylight saving time is observed from the first Sunday in April until the last Sunday in October.

Business and Shopping Hours

San Francisco maintains business hours that are fairly standard throughout the US: 9 AM to 5 PM, Mondays through Fridays. Although banking hours usually are weekdays from 9 AM to 3 PM, many banks stay open later (until 5 or 6 PM) at least one day a week and some offer Saturday morning hours as well. Retail stores usually are open weekdays from 9:30 or 10 AM to 7 or 8 PM, Saturdays until 6 or 7 PM, and many also are open on Sundays (usually from about noon to 5 or 6 PM). Department stores and malls may stay open until 8 or 9 PM at least one day a week.

Mail

San Francisco's main post office (1300 Evans Ave., San Francisco, CA 94188; phone: 415-550-6500) provides window service weekdays from 7 AM to 8:30 PM, and Saturdays from 7 AM to 2 PM; self-service stamp machines are available 24 hours a day in the lobby. Other branches include the *Gateway Station* post office (1 Embarcadero Center, San Francisco, CA 94111; phone: 415-550-6500), which is open weekdays from 8:30 AM to 5:30 PM, and the branch at *Macy's* (170 O'Farrell St. at Union Square, San Francisco, CA 94108; phone: 415-956-3570), which is open weekdays from 10 AM to 5:30 PM, Saturdays from 9 AM to 4:30 PM, and Sundays from 11 AM to 5 PM. It's worth visiting the *Rincon Finance* post office (180 Steuart St., San Francisco, CA 94105; phone: 415-543-3340) just to see this restored 1930s structure; it is open weekdays from 7 AM to 6 PM, and Saturdays from 9 AM to 2 PM. The *Civic Center* post office (101 Hyde St., San Francisco, CA 94142; phone: 415-441-8329) handles General Delivery mail only, and is open weekdays from 9 AM to 5:30 PM (until 7 PM on Thursdays) and Saturdays from 10 AM to 3 PM. For other branches, call the main post office or check the yellow pages.

Stamps also are available at most hotel desks and from public vending machines. For rapid, overnight delivery to other cities, use *Express Mail* (available at post offices), *Federal Express* (phone: 800-238-5355), or *DHL Worldwide Express* (phone: 800-225-5345).

You can have mail sent to you care of your hotel (marked "Guest Mail, Hold for Arrival") or to the *Civic Center* post office (sent "c/o General Delivery" to the address above). Some *American Express* offices in San Francisco also will hold mail for customers ("c/o Client Letter Service"); information is provided in their pamphlet *Travelers' Companion.*

Telephone

The area code for San Francisco, Marin, and south to Los Altos is 415; Oakland, Berkeley, and the rest of the East Bay area are in the 510 area code. To make a long-distance call, dial 1 + the area code + the local number. The nationwide number for information is 555-1212; for local information, you also can dial 411. If you need a number in another area code, dial 1 + the area code + 555-1212. (If you don't know the area code, dial 555-1212 or 411 for directory assistance.) The nationwide number for emergency assistance is 911.

Although you can use a telephone company calling card number on any phone, pay phones that take major credit cards (*American Express, MasterCard, Visa,* and so on) are increasingly common. Also available are combined telephone calling/bank credit cards, such as the *AT&T Universal Card* (PO Box 44167, Jacksonville, FL 32231-4167; phone: 800-423-4343). Similarly, *Sprint* (8140 Ward Pkwy., Kansas City, MO 64114; phone: 800-

THE-MOST or 800-800-USAA) offers the *VisaPhone* program, through which you can add phone card privileges to your existing *Visa* card. Companies offering long-distance phone cards without additional credit card privileges include *AT&T* (phone: 800-CALL-ATT), *Executive Telecard International* (4260 E. Evans Ave., Suite 6, Denver, CO 80222; phone: 800-950-3800), *MCI* (323 Third St. SE, Cedar Rapids, IA 52401; phone: 800-444-4444; and 12790 Merit Dr., Dallas, TX 75251; phone: 800-444-3333), *Metromedia Communications* (1 International Center, 100 NE Loop 410, San Antonio, TX 78216; phone: 800-275-0200), and *Sprint* (address above).

Hotels routinely add surcharges to the cost of phone calls made from their rooms. Long-distance telephone services that may help you avoid this added expense are provided by a number of companies, including *AT&T* (International Information Service, 635 Grant St., Pittsburgh, PA 15219; phone: 800-874-4000), *MCI* (address above), *Metromedia Communications* (address above), and *Sprint* (address above). Note that even when you use such long-distance services, some hotels still may charge a fee for line usage.

Useful resources for travelers include the *AT&T 800 Travel Directory* (phone: 800-426-8686 for orders), the *Toll-Free Travel & Vacation Information Directory* (Pilot Books, 103 Cooper St., Babylon, NY 11702; phone: 516-422-2225; fax: 516-422-2227), and *The Phone Booklet* (Scott American Corporation, PO Box 88, W. Redding, CT 06896; no phone).

Medical Aid

In an emergency: Dial 911 for assistance, 0 for an operator, or go directly to the emergency room of the nearest hospital.

Hospitals

St. Francis Memorial Hospital (900 Hyde St.; phone: 415-353-6000).
San Francisco General Hospital (1001 Potrero Ave.; phone: 415-206-8000).

24-Hour Pharmacies

Walgreens (3201 Divisadero St. at Lombard St.; phone: 415-931-6415 for general information; 415-931-9971 for pharmacy).
Walgreens (498 Castro St.; phone: 415-861-3136).

Additional Resources

International SOS Assistance (PO Box 11568, Philadelphia, PA 19116; phone: 800-523-8930 or 215-244-1500; fax: 215-244-2227).
Medic Alert Foundation (2323 Colorado Ave., Turlock, CA 95382; phone: 800-ID-ALERT or 209-668-3333; fax: 209-669-2495).
Travel Care International (*Eagle River Airport,* PO Box 846, Eagle River, WI 54521; phone: 800-5-AIR-MED or 715-479-8881; fax: 715-479-8178).

Legal Aid

If you don't have, or cannot reach, your own attorney, most cities offer legal referral services maintained by county bar associations. These services ensure that anyone in need of legal representation gets it and can match you with a local attorney. In San Francisco, contact the *San Francisco Bar Association Lawyer Referral Service* (685 Market St., Suite 700, San Francisco, CA 94105; phone: 415-764-1616; fax: 415-546-9223). If you must appear in court, you are entitled to court-appointed representation if you can't obtain a lawyer or can't afford one.

For Further Information

Tourist information is available from the *San Francisco Convention and Visitors Bureau, Visitor Information Center* (900 Market St., San Francisco, CA 94103; phone: 415-391-2000; fax: 415-362-7323; mailing address: PO Box 6977, San Francisco, CA 94101) and the *California Trade and Commerce Agency, Division of Tourism* (801 K St., Suite 1600, Sacramento, CA 95814; phone: 800-GO-CALIF or 916-322-2881; fax: 916-322-3402; mailing address: PO Box 1499, Sacramento, CA 95814). For additional sources of tourist information for San Francisco, see *Sources and Resources* in THE CITY.

The City

San Francisco

Evangelist Billy Graham once stated publicly, "The Bay Area is so beautiful I hesitate to preach about heaven while I'm here." There are few earthbound human beings who are not similarly struck by the splendor of San Francisco. Residents are in love with it; visitors develop instant crushes. A less famous visitor once commented: "I feel sorry for children born here. How sad to grow up and find out the whole world isn't like this."

Any place that can give pause to Billy Graham must be a remarkable piece of geography. And so San Francisco is. Shaped something like a crooked thumb pointing north, the city occupies a hilly peninsula of 47 square miles. On its western border is the Pacific Ocean; to the east is huge, beautiful San Francisco Bay. The waters of the bay join the Pacific through the narrow northern strait that the *Golden Gate Bridge* spans so spectacularly. When the bay fills with fog, as it often does, the bridge becomes a single strand of lights riding over clouds. By choosing an inland suburb or an area along the coast, residents can have either the Sunbelt warmth of California's eternal spring or the sharper, foggier weather of the shoreline.

The city's climate is universally desirable for walking, if you can handle some incredibly steep hills. Even casual strollers can chance upon hidden lanes, small houses circled by picket fences and surrounded by large commercial buildings, stately Victorian façades, stunning murals and other public art, and historical plaques. Grant Avenue provides a tour of Chinatown; Columbus, a glimpse of Italian North Beach and the birthplace of the Beat Generation; and Post Street, a taste of San Francisco's fashionable shops and art galleries.

To live uphill in any part of town is more prestigious than downhill, and to live on a famous hill tops all. Nob Hill, originally the home of railroad and mining nabobs and now the site of several of the city's luxury hotels, is a most elegant address, and Russian Hill offers renowned views of the city and the bay. Along Telegraph Hill's eastern side, Filbert and Greenwich Streets create a series of steps that become wooden sidewalks fronting New England–style cottages, surrounded by gardens and filled with an impressive quiet.

For a city so generously endowed with views, vistas, and vantage points, San Francisco took its time being discovered. Explorers seeking a northern strait and new lands, among them Sir Francis Drake and Juan Rodríguez Cabrillo, sailed up and down the California coast without spying the great, but hidden, inner bay. In 1769 a Spanish land expedition led by Gaspar de Portolá blundered onto San Francisco Bay on a trek north from Mexico. Their goal had been Monterey, and their excitement at discovering one of the world's finest natural harbors was exceeded only by their confusion. The discovery, once made, did not go unexplored. In 1775 another Spaniard,

Juan Manuel de Ayala, sailed through the rugged portals that had hidden the bay for so long, and for the first time the full potential of the inlet was realized.

Soon after the area was fully incorporated into Spain's American empire when Father Francisco Palou built *Misión Dolores.* San Francisco was an early center for the Pacific fur trade, and the 19th century brought New England whalers, Russian trappers, and, when gold was discovered at Sutter's Mill in 1848, nearly everyone else and his brother. By 1850 the population of San Francisco had grown from 900 to 25,000—prompting Will Rogers to observe almost a century later that it was "the city that never was a town." (The population is approximately 725,000 today.) Ten years after the gold strike, silver was found in the Comstock Lode, and San Francisco was caught in a second wave of prosperity that established it as the financial capital of the West. While Levi Strauss made a minor fortune providing miners with denim workwear, Leland Stanford, Charles Crocker, Collis P. Huntington, and Mark Hopkins financed the transcontinental railroad.

In many ways this history influences the city's character today. The Gold Rush brought adventurers from around the world; they were violent, hard men, but they lived together with a certain graceless tolerance. The Chinese came to the city, followed by the Japanese, Russians, Greeks, Mexicans, Filipinos, Irish, and Italians—all settling in larger and smaller communities over the years. The result is an admirable harmony and a kind of hodge-podge culture both pleasing and natural: In what other city is the longtime chef of the town's best pizza parlor Chinese? The basis for this culture is respect and tolerance among individual citizens. The city gives birth to new lifestyles, in part because the civic body politic doesn't get choleric over diversity. It is a center of gay life, for example, and gays are a vital component of the city's mainstream.

Its history probably also has helped make San Francisco a city of survivors. After the October 1989 earthquake (which measured a jarring 6.9 on the Richter scale), cable cars were running the next day, and underground transportation never stopped at all. The visible reminders of the quake were few: a collapsed highway section; a gap in the upper level of the Bay Bridge; a few unsafe buildings shut down. With the help of civic support, just a short time after the disaster, the city looked its elegant self again.

Most experts agree that San Francisco withstood the shock because of the most stringent earthquake building code in the country—and the spunk of its citizens. The Marina district, hardest hit by the quake, still is considered a desirable place to live. In general the people of this city just swept up the shards and stayed in town, undeterred. Consider it an example of San Franciscan mettle: In this city of hills, full buses occasionally have trouble negotiating the steepest inclines. A bus driver with a full load may be forced to stop before beginning an ascent, to ask a few passengers to get off. Remarkably enough, some always do. Though absolutely true, this also is a parable of sorts, a conundrum to contemplate when standing on the Golden Gate Promenade. From there you will see the fine spires of the bridge, with the golden dome of the *Palace of Fine Arts* shining below, and in the distance, framing the picture, the blue Pacific. If that's not a sight worth getting off the bus for, you're just not resident material.

San Francisco At-a-Glance

SEEING THE CITY

Coit Tower, on the summit of Telegraph Hill, offers a spectacular panorama of San Francisco and the surrounding area: To the north are the waterfront and San Francisco Bay, the *Golden Gate Bridge,* Alcatraz Island, and on the far shore, Sausalito; downtown San Francisco lies to the south; to the east are Berkeley and the East Bay hills; and Nob Hill and Russian Hill rise to the west. The tower itself, a 212-foot cylindrical column built in 1933 with funds from a bequest by local eccentric and socialite Lillie Coit "to add beauty to the city she loved," is a striking landmark against the skyline. Inside are restored Depression-era frescoes depicting scenes of California in political, economic, and social vignettes. Open daily. Admission charge to view the lobby frescoes and ride the elevator to the top of the tower. (From Lombard St. follow Telegraph Hill Blvd. to the top; phone: 362-0808.) Twin Peaks, at nearly 1,000 feet, is the city's highest vantage point. (Follow Twin Peaks Blvd. to the top.) Several cocktail lounges offer fine views, too; among the highest, at 779 feet, is the *Carnelian Room,* the restaurant (don't go for the food) and bar atop the Bank of America building, which are open nightly for dinner and on Sundays for brunch (555 California St.; phone: 433-7500). Another unsurpassed 360° panorama is afforded from the *Top of the Mark* lounge of the *Mark Hopkins Inter-Continental* hotel (see *Checking In*).

SPECIAL PLACES

San Francisco is a compact city and easy to get around. Most of the attractions are concentrated within a few areas, and the mild weather year-round makes walking pleasant, but you can sightsee by almost anything that rides, flies, or floats, from cable cars and their motorized facsimiles to buses, bicycles, carriages, trains, boats, helicopters, and hot-air balloons to a beautifully preserved DC-3. *Riders Guide Trips on Tape* (484 Lake Park Ave., Suite 255, Oakland, CA 94610; phone: 510-653-2553) has audiocassettes for do-it-yourself touring between Big Sur and the Napa and Sonoma Valleys, including San Francisco. The best way to see San Francisco is on foot. *City Guides* (phone: 557-4266) offers free neighborhood walking tours (every day except Mondays and Fridays) that highlight the city's historical diversity. For example the "Gold Rush City" trek explores the haunts of the original 49ers, and in Haight-Ashbury remnants of the 196Cs are still evident in the psychedelic street attire worn by diehards. (There are schedules at city libraries, or send a self-addressed, stamped envelope to *Friends of the Library, Main Library, Civic Center,* San Francisco, CA 94102.) The history of the gold miners that once flooded this town and their legendary vices—gambling, drinking, and women—is traced by *A. M. Walking Tours* (phone: 928-5965) through Nob Hill, Chinatown, the old Barbary Coast, Union Square, and Maiden Lane. "Cruisin' the Castro" is a walking tour of "the heart of gay America" (Castro Street); contact Trevor Hailey (375 Lexington St.; phone: 550-8110). *Wok Wiz Chinatown Walking Tours* (750 Kearny St., Suite 800; phone: 355-9657) provides an insider's view of this city within the city—with stops at Chinese markets, herbal shops, a pastry shop that makes rice noodles, an art gallery, a tea shop, and along the narrow streets and alleys of Chinatown for a dim sum lunch.

And finally, for those who prefer to go it afoot on their own, be sure to follow our favorite paths in DIRECTIONS.

DOWNTOWN

CIVIC CENTER This 15-square-block area contains the best collection of Beaux Arts–style buildings in America. Among the buildings are *City Hall,* a notable example of Renaissance grandeur with a 300-foot-high dome; the *War Memorial Opera House,* site of the signing of the UN Charter in 1945 and current home of the *San Francisco Opera* and *Ballet;* the *Bill Graham Civic Auditorium,* scene of cultural and political events since 1915; and the modern *Louise M. Davies Symphony Hall.* The *War Memorial Veterans Building* houses the *San Francisco Museum of Modern Art* (see *Museums*). Wednesdays and Sundays look for the *Heart of the City Farmers' Market* (at the eastern edge of the *Civic Center*), a colorful place rife with exotic fruits and vegetables. Bounded by Franklin, Golden Gate, Leavenworth, and Hayes Streets, the *Civic Center* is a good place to start the *49-Mile Drive,* a well-marked trail that takes in many of the city's highlights. Just follow the blue, white, and orange sea gull signs.

UNION SQUARE Right in the shopping area, Union Square offers a respite from the crowds of people (though not from the hordes of pigeons and panhandlers). You can feed the birds and relax on the benches in good weather. The elegant *Westin St. Francis* hotel is on the west side of the square, while the surrounding area contains sidewalk flower stands and the city's finest department stores and shops. One of the most interesting of these is *Gump's,* with a beautiful collection of jade among its many rare imports (250 Post St.; phone: 982-1616). Bordered by Geary, Post, Powell, and Stockton Sts. For more information see *Walk 2: Union Square/Nob Hill* in DIRECTIONS.

EMBARCADERO CENTER Between the financial district and the waterfront, this 10-acre area of shopping malls, restaurants, hotels, and offices features several notable sculptures, including the controversial *Vaillancourt Fountain* (100 abstractly arranged concrete boxes with water spouting from them, often described by locals as the intestines of a square dog) and a 60-foot sculpture by the late Louise Nevelson. At the foot of Market St.

SAN FRANCISCO WATERFRONT Once a world class working port, the city's waterfront now is more like a world class promenade thanks to *The Embarcadero.* Outstanding views of Treasure Island, the light-festooned Bay Bridge, and distant East Bay Bridge draw an admiring audience. Pier 7 is a walkway out over the bay for strolling, fishing, or sightseeing. A farmers' market held on Saturdays at the foot of Market Street bustles with people and is chockablock with stalls of fresh produce, bread, and ready-to-eat food from local restaurants. Walking south along *The Embarcadero* you pass the *Harbor Court Hotel*'s brick façade, the *Gordon Biersch Brewery* bar and restaurant at Harrison Street, and the *Embarko* restaurant in the Bay Village complex at Brannon Street. The waterfront area runs about half a mile along *The Embarcadero,* from Market Street south to Brannon Street.

CHINATOWN One of the largest Chinese communities outside Asia, Chinatown is an intriguing 24-block enclave of pagoda-roofed buildings, excellent restaurants, and fine import shops featuring ivory carvings and jade jewelry; there are also several temples and museums here. Grant Avenue is the main thoroughfare—enter through an archway crowned by a dragon (Grant at Bush St.). It's best to go on foot or take the California Street cable car, because the area is too congested for easy parking. If you must drive, try the *Portsmouth Square Garage* (at Kearny St., north of Clay St.). The *Old St. Mary's Church* (Grant Ave. and California St.), built in 1854 of granite from China and bricks from New England, is the city's oldest cathedral. It survived the 1906 and 1989 earthquakes, perhaps because of its warning on the façade above the clock dial: "Son Observe the Time and Fly from Evil." More words of wisdom, as well as regional artifacts, including tiny slippers used for the bound feet of Oriental ladies, pipes from old Chinatown opium dens, and photographs of some famed telephone operators who memorized the names and numbers of 2,400 Chinatown residents in the old days, can be found at the *Chinese Historical Society of America*'s museum, the largest Chinese-American collection in the US (650 Commercial St., between Kearny and Montgomery; phone: 391-1188). Open Tuesdays through Saturdays, afternoons only. No admission charge. For information on walking tours of Chinatown, contact the *Chinese Cultural Center,* Tuesdays through Saturdays (750 Kearny St., inside the *Holiday Inn;* phone: 986-1822), or *Wok Wiz Chinatown Walking Tours* (see above). For more information see *Walk 4: Chinatown* in DIRECTIONS.

NORTH BEACH There is no longer a beach here, but this traditional neighborhood remains colorful and diverse—mostly Italian, Basque, and Chinese. The area's great for strolling and eating—bakeries and bread shops sell cannoli, rum babas, marzipan, and panettone (a sweet bread filled with raisins and candied fruit). Numerous restaurants and cafés serve anything from espresso and cappuccino to complete dinners. One of the best times of year to visit North Beach is in early June, during the street bazaar, when local artists display their wares along Upper Grant Avenue. Other times numerous galleries and studios exhibit crafts, paintings, jewelry, and unusual clothing. Washington Square is a nice place to sit in the sun or have lunch with the locals under the statue—ironically, not of the square's namesake—of Benjamin Franklin (Columbus and Union Sts.). North Beach extends north and northwest from Chinatown to Bay Street. For more information see *Walk 3: North Beach* in DIRECTIONS.

JAPAN CENTER This modern complex, the focal point of culture and trade for San Francisco's substantial Japanese community, is in the area where the Japanese lived before World War II. The five-acre complex contains movie theaters, tea houses, restaurants, sushi and tempura bars, art galleries, shops selling everything from pearls to stereo equipment, and a school that offers classes in Japanese doll making and flower arranging. With its five-tier *Peace Pagoda* in the center of a reflecting pool, the elegantly landscaped Peace Plaza is the scene of the April *Cherry Blossom Festival* and traditional Japanese celebrations, like the *Mochi-Pounding Ceremony* (in which much preparation and even more pounding result in delicious rice cakes). Speaking of pounding, the *Kabuki Hot Springs and Japanese Spa* offers shiatsu massage, traditional Japanese baths, whirlpool baths, saunas, steambaths, and other services; the works will leave you feeling as fresh and crisp as a newly made rice cake (1750 Geary Blvd.; phone: 922-6000). The *Kinokuniya* bookstore, a large, well-appointed place with books and periodicals in English as well as Japanese, offers browsers an unparalleled look at contemporary Japan. The area is bounded by Laguna, Fillmore, Geary, and Post Streets.

FISHERMAN'S WHARF AND VICINITY

FISHERMAN'S WHARF This rambling waterfront section—getting tackier by the year—is both the center of the commercial fishing industry and California's largest tourist attraction after *Disneyland*. On the wharf at Jefferson Street, you walk through an open-air fish market. Locals find it more convenient to shop for fish in their own neighborhoods, but you can create the ultimate urban picnic by buying a loaf of freshly baked sourdough bread at *Boudin's* bakery (156 Jefferson St.; phone: 928-1849) and adding Dungeness crab purchased at one of the numerous sidewalk stalls. The boats return in the afternoon and hoist their crates of fish onto the pier at the foot of Jones and Leavenworth Streets. The wharf restaurants often are crowded and expensive, but try the huge *Alioto's No. 8;* the menu has been upgraded with Sicilian seafood recipes, and the cappuccino is as good as the best in Italy (at the foot of Taylor St.; phone: 673-0183). The area has many outlets selling hand-crafted items. For more information see *Walk 5: The Other Waterfront* in DIRECTIONS.

PIER 39 Reconstructed with wood salvaged from other (demolished) piers and looking more like Gloucester, Massachusetts, than the West Coast, *Pier 39* is a popular entertainment complex on the northern waterfront. A pleasant hour or two can be spent moving with the crowds through the plethora of shops—craft, bakery, import, clothing, specialty, toy, jewelry, camera, fine food, crystal and silver, and many others. Meanwhile mimes, jugglers, and other street performers provide continuous entertainment. For lunch or dinner, there's an international roster of restaurants from which to choose—French, Italian, Chinese, Swiss; grab a bite at one of the numerous stand-up, take-out fresh seafood booths; or simply indulge your sweet tooth at *Breyer's Ice Cream.* The *Eagle Café* (phone: 433-3689) still attracts enough longshoremen to lend a working class aura not otherwise evident in this part of the waterfront. Children can run off excess energy at the pier's playground and park or take a ride on the double-decker Venetian carousel at the end of the pier; sailors and fishermen can charter boats at the marina; and landlubbers can watch the more than 300 sea lions that sun themselves on the docks. *Pier 39* is on *The Embarcadero,* just east of *Fisherman's Wharf.* (There's a parking garage across the way on Beach St.)

SAN FRANCISCO MARITIME NATIONAL HISTORICAL PARK A huge, ship-shape building at the foot of Polk Street, the park's *National Maritime Museum* is a treasure trove of memorabilia documenting shipping development from Gold Rush days to the present with photographs, figureheads, massive anchors, shipwreck relics, and beautiful model ships. Open daily. No admission charge (*Aquatic Park;* phone: 556-3002). Berthed off nearby Hyde Street Pier, three old ships welcome the public aboard. The *Balclutha* was a British cargo ship that rounded Cape Horn 17 times carrying rice and wine to San Francisco, worked as an Alaskan salmon trader, and even did a stint in Hollywood as a rather oversize prop in films. The *Eureka* used to shuttle passengers and cars across the bay during the early decades of this century. The antique automobiles displayed on deck are sure to delight car buffs. Aboard the schooner *CA Thayer,* old salts sing chanteys some evenings. All open daily. Admission charge (phone: 556-1871). Also here—though unavailable for boarding—are the *Alma,* a scow schooner built in 1891; the *Eppleton Hall,* a 1914 British tugboat; and the *Hercules,* a 1907 oceangoing steam tug that hauled logs to mills down the coast. *The Maritime Store* is full of books about the sea plus maps and posters (phone: 775-BOOK).

PIER 45/USS PAMPANITO A project of the *National Maritime Museum Association.* On display are historical photographs of this World War II submarine, including its role in the sinking of two Japanese ships with 2,000 British and Australian POWs aboard and the rescue of 73 survivors two days later. On board a narrated tape guides visitors through the operations of a submersible, where every inch of space had to be put to life-and-death use. Open daily. Admission charge. Pier 45 (phone: 929-0202).

BAY CRUISES AND ATTRACTIONS The *Blue & Gold Fleet* (*Pier 39*; phone: 705-5444) offers daily cruises, and evenings from April through December passengers can dine and dance across the bay. From the north side of the *Ferry Building* (located at the foot of Market St.), relive the days before the bridge was built by sailing to Oakland and Alameda. The *Red & White Fleet* uses Piers 41 and 43½, near *Fisherman's Wharf*, for its cruises and services to the north bay (phone: 546-2805 or 800-229-2784). Choose among Alcatraz (reserve ahead in summer and on holiday weekends), Sausalito, and Tiburon, with optional tours to the redwoods at *Muir Woods National Monument* and to Vallejo, with bus extension to *Marine World Africa USA* (phone: 707-644-4000; fax 707-644-0241). The latter features an enormous and exotic collection of sea, air, and land creatures and visitor participant activities such as playing tug-of-war with the elephants, giraffe feeding, getting close to prairie dogs and pygmy goats in the petting *kraal*, and learning about newborn animals like Bengal tiger cubs in the *Animal Nursery;* the marine part includes a killer whale and dolphin show, a shark habitat with a see-through tunnel, and a seal cove; and a new section includes a *Jurassic Park*-inspired *Dinosaurs!* exhibit. Admission charge is included in the cruise fee. Or, if you want to go on your own, *Marine World Africa USA* can also be reached from downtown San Francisco via high-speed catamaran in one hour, by car in 30 minutes, or by public transport; call the number above for more information. The *Red & White Fleet* also offers a three-winery cruise visit to the Napa Valley. And *Hornblower Dining Yachts* offers brunch, lunch, and dinner on its sails around the bay (Pier 33; phone: 394-8900).

ALCATRAZ ISLAND This famed escape-proof former federal penitentiary stands out grimly in the bay, 1½ miles from *Fisherman's Wharf.* Such notorious criminals as Al Capone, "Machine Gun" Kelly, and Doc Barker never returned from their stays here. The prison was closed in 1963 because of exorbitant operating costs and has been open to the public since 1973. The *National Park Service* runs tours of the prison block, where you see the "dark holes" in which rebellious prisoners were confined in solitude and the tiny steel-barred cells. Two-hour tours depart daily on the *Red & White Fleet* (see *Bay Cruises,* above) on a first-come, first-served basis; tickets may be purchased in advance (strongly recommended for the summer and holiday weekends) through *Ticketron* (phone: 510-762-2277). Ferries sail from Pier 41.

GHIRARDELLI SQUARE Pronounced *Gear-a-del*li. Originally a woolen mill that turned out Union Army uniforms during the Civil War, then later a chocolate factory, the stately, landmark, red brick buildings here now house import shops that sell anything from Persian rugs to Chinese kites, plus outdoor cafés, art galleries, and fine restaurants. The *Mandarin* (phone: 673-8812) serves excellent Chinese food; *McCormick & Kuleto's* (phone: 929-1730) serves seafood in a flashy setting with stunning bay views; but perhaps sweetest of all is the *Ghirardelli Chocolate Manufactory* (phone: 474-3938), where you can watch chocolate being made and then eat the spoils afterward. If you're truly inspired, try the Golden Gate banana split. Open daily, on weekends until midnight. Bounded by Beach, Larkin, North Point, and Polk Sts.

THE CANNERY Inspired by *Ghirardelli Square,* this former Del Monte cannery is now a three-level arcade featuring chic boutiques, restaurants, and the *Museum of the City of San Francisco* (see *Museums*). Street musicians and mimes strut their stuff in the olive tree–shaded central courtyard. Open daily. Bounded by Beach, Leavenworth, and Jefferson Sts.

LOMBARD STREET Take the time to appreciate the residential façades and color-ful flowers that line what is often referred to as the most twisting urban street in the world. (Also see *Quintessential San Francisco* in DIVERSIONS.)

GOLDEN GATE—FROM THE PROMENADE TO THE PARK

GOLDEN GATE PROMENADE This 3½-mile shoreline trail is among the most spec-tacular walks (or jogging paths) in America. You meander from *Aquatic Park* past wind-shaped Monterey cypress, eroding rocky points, a classy yacht harbor in front of the *St. Francis Yacht Club,* a grassy park beside an old cobbled seawall, all the while approaching that ultimate span, the *Golden Gate Bridge.* A number of interesting museums line the way. *Fort Point,* completed in 1861 as the West Coast's only Civil War outpost, is now a *National Historic Site.* Closed Mondays and Tuesdays. No admission charge (at the base of the *Golden Gate Bridge,* Presidio; phone: 556-1693). The *Presidio Army Museum,* established in 1776 as a Spanish garrison and housed in the *Old Station Hospital,* has artifacts tracing its history. Closed Mondays and Tuesdays. No admission charge (Lincoln Blvd. and Funston Ave.; phone: 556-0856). Most unusual is the *Palace of Fine Arts,* a grand Beaux Arts building constructed for the 1915 *Panama-Pacific International Exposition.* It houses the *Exploratorium,* a collection of 800 displays on sci-ence, technology, and the reaches and limits of human perception (see *Museums*).

GOLDEN GATE BRIDGE The loftiest and one of the longest single-span suspension bridges ever constructed, the bright-orange *Golden Gate* marked its golden (50th) anniversary in 1987 with a huge celebration that culminated in the permanent lighting of its twin towers. To enjoy a stunning view, follow the handicapped-accessible walk up to the toll plaza level, where you'll also find gardens landscaped with native flowering plants. From here you have several options: You can catch a bus back downtown; turn around and walk back with the view of the city skyline accompanying you all the way; or fol-low in the footsteps of great coast trekkers across the bridge and beyond— north along trails on the ridges and shoreline for 60 miles to Tomales Point. Yes, you can walk across the bridge (and under it); if you are driving, take the very first exit across the bridge, park, and enjoy the terrific view of San Francisco. Also see *Walk 5: The Other Waterfront* in DIRECTIONS.

SAN FRANCISCO ZOO *Gorilla World* and an ultramodern $7-million *Primate Discovery Center* make a visit here particularly worthwhile. More than a thousand birds and animals can be viewed on foot or from aboard the motorized tour train. Adjacent to the main zoo is the *Children's Zoo,* a seven-acre nursery where children can stroke barnyard animals or watch baby lions being bottle fed. An outstanding *Insect Zoo* brings kids face to face with an impressive collection of creepy crawlers. The spectacular primate center has dozens of exotic and/or endangered species, as well as hands-on experiments and informative, fun-to-do computer/slide programs. Open daily. Admission charge. Sloat Blvd. and 45th Ave. (phone: 753-7080).

GOLDEN GATE PARK Developed from a thousand acres of rolling sand dunes, *Golden Gate Park* has all the amenities of a large recreation area: bike paths, hiking and equestrian trails, three lakes (where you can sail model boats or practice casting), sports fields, and a 25-acre meadow. The park also features a rose garden, the lovely *John McLaren Rhododendron Dell,* the *Strybing Arboretum and Botanical Gardens*—over 70 acres rich with 5,000 species of plants and trees from all over the world—and the *Conservatory of Flowers,* a greenhouse with lush tropical growth. Arboretum and conservatory open daily. No admission charge to arboretum. (Along Martin Luther King Jr. Dr. and John F. Kennedy Dr., respectively.) The *Japanese Tea Garden* is a masterpiece of Oriental landscaping. Open daily. Admission charge. (At the intersection of Martin Luther King Jr. Dr. and Tea Garden Dr., just west of the *de Young Museum.*) No such lyrical setting could be complete without music, and the *Music Concourse* offers free open-air *Municipal Band* concerts on Sunday afternoons at 1 when the weather is good (between the *de Young Museum* and the *California Academy of Science;* see *Museums* for both). For more information, see *Walk 7: Golden Gate Park* in DIRECTIONS and *Glorious Gardens* in DIVERSIONS.

SOUTH OF MARKET STREET

SOMA Formerly the city's gritty warehouse district (the name stands for "South of Market"), this area has been transformed into a vibrant, lived-in, artistic neighborhood of street markets and performers, shops, galleries, small theaters, gay bars, and nightclubs. Even as housing prices have veered upward, it remains one of San Francisco's most accessible, most colorful districts. Some once-elegant residential buildings still stand on Third Street, and living lofts are slowly being fashioned out of the former warehouses. South Park, at the heart of the district, is flanked by several clubs and restaurants. SoMa also is home to the *Moscone Convention Center* (named in memory of the assassinated San Francisco mayor) and the adjacent *Center for the Arts at Yerba Buena Gardens* (see below). There are also enough discount clothing outlets and boutiques to satiate even the most obsessed shopper (see *Shopping*). *Shopper Stopper* (PO Box 535, Sebastopol, CA 95473; phone: 707-829-1597) offers a 6½-hour shopping tour of the area, stopping at wholesalers not usually open to the public. The area is roughly bounded by Market, Embarcadero, China Basin, and Division Streets.

CENTER FOR THE ARTS AT YERBA BUENA GARDENS A sprawling complex of galleries, theaters, gardens, a walk-behind fountain, plus a café and gift shop, the center showcases the city's culture and traditions. Offerings on this theme run the gamut from painting to electronic music, from ballet to video, from sculpture to CD-ROM. A limited number of discounted tickets go on sale at 11 AM Tuesdays at the *Center for the Arts's Ticket Office* (phone: 978-2787); each person is allowed to purchase two tickets to selected performances the same week. 701 Mission St., between Third and Fourth Sts.

EXTRA SPECIAL

Within an hour's drive of San Francisco (north along US 101, east on Rte. 37, then north on Rte. 121) begins the number one wine-producing region in the US, the gently rolling Sonoma County and, beyond, the Napa Valley. (See *Visitable Vineyards* in DIVERSIONS for the most interesting wineries for tours and tastings.) Many eateries in this area offer intoxicating dining. *Château Souverain* (400 Souverain Rd.; phone: 707-433-3141) in Geyserville, for example, serves a cornmeal polenta with tomato fondue. The mild weather encourages not only grape production but outdoor activity. Pick up some bread and cheese along Highway 29 en route to *Bothe–Napa Valley State Park*. Its thousand acres of broad-leaved trees, pines, and redwoods are a lovely backdrop for picnicking, biking, and swimming in summer. In Yountville you can shop on three levels at *Vintage 1879,* a group of specialty stores housed in a renovated brick warehouse, or take a hot-air balloon ride (contact *Adventures Aloft;* phone: 707-255-8688). Stop at *The Diner* (6476 Washington St., Yountville; phone: 707-944-2626) for lunch, dinner, or a wonderful mocha milk shake. *St. Helena's Terra* restaurant (1345 Railroad Ave., St. Helena; phone: 707-963-8931) combines the cooking techniques of several cultures to come up with creative and outstanding meals. At *Tra Vigne* restaurant (1050 Charter Oak Ave., St. Helena; phone: 707-963-4444) dine alfresco on northern Italian fare. Calistoga, to the north, is a health spa with its own "Old Faithful," a 60-foot geyser of steam erupting about every 40 minutes. *Dr. Wilkinson's Hot Springs* (1507 Lincoln Ave., Calistoga; phone: 707-942-4102) offers refreshing mud baths and mineral whirlpools. If time permits, try one of the Napa Valley's charming bed and breakfast establishments, such as *La Residence* (4066 St. Helena Hwy. N., Napa, CA 94558; phone: 707-253-0337). *Meadowood Resort* (900 Meadowood La., St. Helena, CA 94574; phone: 707-963-3646) and *Auberge du Soleil* (180 Rutherford Hill Rd., Rutherford, CA 94573; phone: 707-963-1211) are both resorts with beautiful rooms and renowned restaurants. Or you may find you don't want to move from

Sonoma County, with its rugged coastline, deep woods, and picturesque farms. There are many charming bed and breakfast accommodations: Off Highway 101, but as peaceful as a sleepy small town, the *Vintners Inn* (4350 Barnes Rd., Santa Rosa, CA 95403; phone: 707-575-7350) is centrally located for visits to the vineyards in both the Sonoma and Napa Valleys. A few steps away is *John Ash & Company* (4330 Barnes Rd., Santa Rosa, CA 95403; phone: 707-527-7687), one of Sonoma's best restaurants. *Piatti* (405 First St. W., on the plaza in Sonoma; phone: 707-996-2351), the popular offspring of the restaurant of the same name in Yountville (6480 Washington St., Yountville, CA 94599; phone: 707-944-2070), offers innovative Italian trattoria fare. If you want the elegance of a 1920s luxury hotel plus a fitness spa, try the *Sonoma Mission Inn & Spa* (PO Box 1447, Sonoma, CA 95476 or 18140 Sonoma Hwy. 12, Boyes Hot Springs, CA 95416; phone: 707-938-9000 or 800-358-9022); smart guests here begin their day with the sourdough French toast in *The Café*. Once a graceful 1800s summer home, *Madrona Manor* (1001 Westside Rd., Healdsburg, CA 95448; phone: 707-433-4231) offers the ambience of life on a country estate. An especially nice way to see the area north of San Francisco is on a one-week cruise in October aboard the *Yorktown Clipper* (*Clipper Cruise Line*, 7711 Bonhomme Ave., St. Louis, MO 63105-1965; phone: 314-727-2929 or 800-325-0010), which includes excursions to Sausalito, Sacramento, and California's wine country. *Special Expeditions* (729 Fifth Ave., New York, NY 10019; phone: 212-765-7740 or 800-762-0003) offers a similar four-day cruise in November, and *Delta Travel* (PO Box 813, W. Sacramento, CA 95691; phone: 916-372-3690) features one- and two-day cruises to the wine country and its environs from May through October.

South of San Francisco and about two hours away (via Rte. 101, then Rte. 156, then Rte. 1, or via the slow, scenic coastal Rte. 1 all the way) lies the Monterey Peninsula, an area rich in history and natural beauty. The town of Monterey was the military capital of California under three flags, and many of its adobe buildings survive in the *State Historic Park*. On Cannery Row, where gift shops and restaurants have taken over defunct sardine canneries, the *Monterey Bay Aquarium* (886 Cannery Row; phone: 408-648-4888) is a spectacular re-creation of the region's marine environment. The peninsula's pine forests and broad white beaches, bright with flowering succulents, are breathtaking. Famous for golf at *Pebble Beach,* the area also attracts nature lovers who come to see monarch butterflies wintering in Pacific Grove, sea otters, seals, and the wild shore lands of *Point Lobos State Preserve,* south of Carmel. In this inexplicably faux-Bavarian resort town is a blessedly Mediterranean retreat with gorgeous gardens, *La Playa* hotel (Camino Real at Eighth, Carmel-by-the-Sea,

CA 93921; phone: 408-624-6476 or 800-582-8900). Close to Monterey, in the heart of the Carmel Valley, is *Stonepine* (150 E. Carmel Valley Rd., Carmel Valley, CA 93924; phone: 408-659-2245), a country French château set on 330 acres 22 miles east of Carmel, an elegant bed and breakfast and sports facility (there are 13 rooms and a cottage, *Paddock House*, available as guest accommodations). It has a large equestrian center with horses for hire on an hourly basis to guests and non-guests; mountain bikes are available only for guests' use (no charge), and there are trails into the surrounding hills, suitable for equestrians and cyclists as well as for hikers. No children under 12 permitted in the château; guests with children can, however, be accommodated in the *Paddock House*.

Sources and Resources

TOURIST INFORMATION

The *San Francisco Convention and Visitors' Bureau* (*Visitor Information Center*, PO Box 429097, San Francisco, CA 94142; phone: 391-2000) is best for brochures, maps, general tourist information, and other assistance. If you write ahead, it will send you (for $2) a valuable package of information, including a three-month calendar of events. Call 391-2001 anytime for the lowdown on what's going on in town. The bureau's downtown *Visitor Information Center* on the lower level of *Hallidie Plaza* (just downstairs from the cable car turntable, at 900 Market St. at Powell St.) provides multilingual services. Contact the California state hotline (phone: 800-TO-CALIF) for maps, calendars of events, health updates, and travel advisories.

LOCAL COVERAGE The *San Francisco Chronicle* is a morning daily; the *San Francisco Examiner,* an evening daily. On Fridays both list events and places to go on weekends. Sundays the two publish a joint edition, including a comprehensive entertainment section, the "Datebook."

San Francisco at Your Feet by Margot Patterson Doss (Grove Press, $12.95) and *San Francisco: The Ultimate Guide* by Randolph Delehanty (Chronicle Books, $14.95) are good walking guides; *San Francisco Access* (HarperCollins, $18) is popular for its clarity and interesting layout. *Travels in San Francisco* by Herbert Gold (Arcade, $8.95) and *Discover America: San Francisco and the Bay Area* (Compass America Guides, $14.95) give practical information on the city's fascinating neighborhoods.

FOOD Consult *Best Restaurants of San Francisco: The San Francisco Chronicle Guide to Fine Dining* (Chronicle Books, $10.95) and *Exploring the Best Ethnic Restaurants of the Bay Area* by Sharon Silva and Frank Viviano (S.F. Focus Books, $9.95).

TELEVISION STATIONS KRON Channel 4–NBC; KPIX Channel 5–CBS; KGO Channel 7–ABC; KQED Channel 9–PBS; KTVU Channel 17–CNN.

RADIO STATIONS AM: KFRC 610 (oldies); KCBS 740 (news); KGO 810 (news/talk); FM: KQED 88.5 (national public radio); KJAZ 92.7 (jazz); KKHI 95.7 (classical).

TELEPHONE The area code for San Francisco, Marin, and south to Los Altos is 415. The area code for Oakland, Berkeley, and the rest of the East Bay area is 510. For further information, see GETTING READY TO GO.

SALES TAX Sales tax is 8.25%; hotel tax is 12%.

GETTING AROUND

BART If you really want to move, this ultramodern, high-speed railway will whisk you from San Francisco to Oakland, Berkeley, Richmond, Concord, Daly City, and Fremont at up to 80 miles an hour. The system is easy to use, with large maps and signboards in each station clarifying routes and fares (which vary according to distance traveled). For information, contact *Bay Area Rapid Transit (BART),* 800 Madison St., Oakland (phone: 788-BART in San Francisco).

BUS Efficient buses serve the entire metropolitan area; maps appear at the front of the yellow pages in the telephone book. *MUNI (Municipal Transit)* Passports ($6 per day, $10 for three days, and $15 per week) are good for rides on *MUNI* buses, streetcars, and cable cars. *MUNI* street and transit maps are available at bookstores for $2. For detailed route information, contact the *Municipal Railway of San Francisco,* 949 Presidio Ave. (phone: 673-MUNI daily during business hours).

CABLE CAR The best way to travel up and over the hills of downtown is aboard these famous trademarks, which are pulled along at 9½ miles an hour. There are three lines, the most scenic being the Powell–Hyde route, which you can pick up at the turntable at Powell and Market Streets. It will take you over both Nob and Russian Hills to gaslit Victorian Park (see *Quintessential San Francisco* in DIVERSIONS).

CAR RENTAL For information on renting a car, see GETTING READY TO GO.

FERRY For outstanding views of the city, ride the *Golden Gate Ferry* (phone: 332-6600) from the terminal under the clock tower at the foot of Market Street. The 30-minute ride to Sausalito (slightly longer to Larkspur) takes you right past Alcatraz and almost within reach of the *Golden Gate Bridge.*

STREETCAR Five lines of the *MUNI Metro* streetcar system run under Market Street, one level above *BART,* and branch off toward various parts of the city. For route information, call 673-MUNI.

TAXI Cabs can be hailed on downtown streets, especially near hotels, or summoned by phone. Major companies are *Luxor Cab* (phone: 282-4141), *Veterans Cab* (phone: 552-1300), and *Yellow Cab* (phone: 626-2345).

LOCAL SERVICES

AUDIOVISUAL EQUIPMENT *McCune Audio/Visual/Video* (phone: 641-1111).

BUSINESS SERVICES More and more hotels are offering in-house business services; see *Checking In.*

DRY CLEANER/TAILOR *Cable Car Tailors* (84 Ellis St.; phone: 781-4636); *Larry So* (456 Montgomery St.; phone: 981-6343); *Paragon* (635 Bush St.; phone: 781-2646).

LIMOUSINE *Carey Nob Hill Limousine* (phone: 468-7550); *Opera Plaza Limousines* (phone: 826-9630).

MECHANICS *Foreign Car Repair,* for imports (6027 Geary Blvd. between 24th and 25th Aves.; phone: 752-8305); *Honda Auto Repair,* for American and Japanese autos (2941 Geary Blvd.; phone: 751-7860); *San Francisco Golden Gate Motors,* for German-built cars (1444 Green St.; phone: 931-9076).

MEDICAL EMERGENCY For information on area hospitals and pharmacies, see GETTING READY TO GO.

MESSENGER SERVICES *PDQ* (phone: 346-4229); *Western Messenger Service* (phone: 864-4100).

PHOTOCOPIES *Blue Print Service Co.,* with overnight service available (149 Second St.; phone: 495-8700); *The Print & Copy Factory,* open 24 hours (2136 Palou Ave.; phone: 641-7500).

POST OFFICES For information on local branch offices, see GETTING READY TO GO.

PROFESSIONAL PHOTOGRAPHER *Gabriel Moulin Studios* (526 Second St.; phone: 541-9454); *Romaine Photography* (Russ Bldg., 235 Montgomery St.; phone: 989-3536).

SECRETARY *Ancha Business Center* (2500 Mason St., inside the *Sheraton at Fisherman's Wharf* hotel; phone: 627-6530); *Headquarters Co.* (phone: 781-5000).

TELECONFERENCE FACILITIES Available in most downtown hotels with business clientele (see *Checking In*).

TRANSLATOR *Berlitz* (180 Montgomery St., 15th Floor; phone: 986-6474); *I.E.C.* (690 Market St.; phone: 781-8555).

WESTERN UNION/TELEX Telegrams (phone: 800-325-6000 to find the location nearest you). For information on money transfers, see GETTING READY TO GO.

SPECIAL EVENTS

San Franciscans know how to throw a party, and anyone lucky enough to be in town during one—which is usually every week—is welcome to join in the fun. Some are big, some are unusual, and everyone has a favorite reason for celebrating. To find out what's happening in any given week, call the *Visitor Information Center* (phone: 391-2000) or check the "Datebook" section of the Sunday *San Francisco Examiner and Chronicle.*

FAVORITE FETES

Chinese New Year For nine days each year, Chinatown is even noisier and more crowded than usual. Fireworks explode day and night; the streets and storefronts are rife with red paper envelopes and other symbols of good luck. Hundreds of thousands of onlookers come to see the parade on the final day, when block-long dragons steered from within by more than a hundred people wind through the narrow streets, leading floats and marching bands to a festival in Portsmouth Square. The final celebration runs from 8 AM to midnight; fireworks are shot off at the end of the parade. The date of the *Chinese New Year* fluctuates from year to year, falling in either January or February. For further information contact the *Chinese Chamber of Commerce* (phone: 982-3000).

Lesbian/Gay Freedom Day Parade San Francisco's large gay community, as well as their friends and supporters, take to the streets on the last Sunday of June every year for this event. Traditionally, the parade begins on Market Street, led by the "Women's Motorcycle Contingent," a group of leather-clad cycling lesbians, and travels along Market to the *Civic Center Plaza.* Costumes run the gamut and, frankly, defy description. The party continues on the plaza, with food, clothing, information booths, and four stages presenting continuous entertainment and speakers. This celebration of a lifestyle is in no way limited to those who practice it. The parade usually begins at 11 AM (phone: 864-FREE).

San Francisco Blues Festival The country's oldest blues festival occurs each year on a long weekend in late September, and features both national and local talent. B. B. King, Etta James, and Robert Cray have been among the many performers at this event, which was launched in 1972. Historian and blues music authority Tom Mazzolini created it as a showcase for the many great and aging blues artists who migrated from the South during World War II to work in the shipyards of the East Bay. After a more humble beginning inside a San Francisco gymnasium, the music now emanates from the *Great Meadow* at *Upper Fort Mason* (enter at Bay Street off Franklin Street) and floats out over San Francisco Bay. Blues fans from all over the world spread their blankets and lawn chairs across the natural amphitheater, listening to the music while sampling barbecue and Cajun cooking and enjoying views of the *Golden Gate Bridge* and the crowds of sailboats. Music plays from 11 AM to 5:30 PM; tickets are available in advance; see below for ticket sales information. Or sample the music in advance at the blues festival's free noontime "kick-off" concert at *Justin Herman Plaza,* located at *Embarcadero Four* at the *Embarcadero Center,* on the Friday before the yearly event (phone: 979-5588).

Carnaval San Francisco This two-day festival is the San Francisco version of *Carnaval* in Rio de Janeiro. Marchers in bright, exotic, erotic costumes wind through the mission district to the festival site on Harrison Street. From the main stage comes Caribbean-style music; another stage is devoted to samba. Food, music, and crafts from South America, Central America, and the Caribbean abound. *Carnaval* is held on *Memorial Day* weekend (phone: 826-1401 for further information).

Other not-to-be-missed special events include the following:

The *Cherry Blossom Festival,* held on two weekends in April at the *Japan Center* (Post and Buchanan Sts.), features traditional tea ceremonies, flower-arranging and doll-making demonstrations, bonsai displays, and performances by folk dancers from Japan. A crosstown parade highlights the events with over 50 Japanese performing groups and intricate floats of shrines and temples.

Fleet Week celebrates the October birthday of the US Navy with a parade of ships under the *Golden Gate Bridge* and several days of open houses on the vessels, plus aerial events, fireworks, and boat rides.

The *Grand National Livestock Exposition, Rodeo and Horse Show,* held in late October and early November at the *Cow Palace* (just south of the city on Geneva Ave., off US 101), is one of the biggest events in the country, with all manner of rodeo events, equestrian competitions, and the best livestock in the West.

MUSEUMS

Many cultures and many crafts merge in San Francisco; East meets West, and each celebrates a long history of fine arts. Museums and galleries here boast ancient Asian arts and emerging contemporary ideas. Note: The *California Palace of the Legion of Honor* in *Lincoln Park*—a memorial to America's World War I dead that houses a fine collection of European art from medieval times through the 20th century—is closed for renovations and scheduled to reopen later this year. Call 863-3330 for further information.

MEMORABLE MUSEUMS

Asian Art Museum Created to accommodate the collection donated by Avery Brundage, this museum is known for the scope of its works, which span a 6,000-year period. More than 500 masterpieces—including the earliest dated bronze Chinese Buddha (AD 338) and a 2,000-year-old bronze rhinoceros wine vessel—are on permanent exhibit. Also on display is one of the world's most extensive collections of Gandharan sculpture (from northern India). Housed in a specially constructed wing of the *de Young Museum* (see below), the *Asian Art Museum* is operated separately. Closed Mondays and Tuesdays. Admission charge (also good for admission to the *de Young Museum* on the same day). Across from the *Music Concourse* in *Golden Gate Park* (phone: 668-7855).

M. H. de Young Memorial Museum An outstanding collection of American art, ranging from the colonial era through the 20th century, and including major contributions by Mr. and Mrs. John D. Rockefeller III, hangs on the walls of the 22 galleries in this fine arts museum. Works by John Singer Sargent, Mary Cassatt, and George Caleb Bingham are among those exhibited. Also featured is art from ancient Egypt, Greece, Oceania, and Africa plus a large textile collection. The *Achenback Foundation for Graphic Arts* is housed here until later this year, when it will return to the *California Palace of the Legion of Honor* (see above). The *de Young* building originally was constructed for the *1894 California Midwinter Exposition,* which was backed and publicized by *San Francisco Chronicle* founder M. H. de Young. Lunch and refreshments are served in the *de Young Café.* Closed Mondays and Tuesdays; lecture tours available on all other days. Admission charge (also good for admission to the *Asian Art Museum* on the same day). *Music Concourse, Golden Gate Park* (phone: 750-3600; 863-3330 for recorded information).

San Francisco Museum of Modern Art California's first museum devoted to modern art moved last year to a $60-million Mario Botta–designed facility across from the *Center for the Arts at Yerba Buena Gardens;* it will open to the public on January 31, 1995. It has a distinguished permanent collection of photography and American abstract expressionist art, with paintings by Jackson Pollock and Clyfford Still, among others. Contemporary works by Bay Area artists such as Wayne Thiebaud and Richard Diebenkorn are likewise exhibited here. In addition to the 20th-century paintings, sculpture, and works on paper, the museum houses a department of architecture and design, and a department focusing on media arts. Music, lectures, and film events are frequently scheduled; there's also a small, selective bookshop and a café. Open daily, on Thursdays until 9 PM. Admission charge; the first Tuesday of every month is free; Thursday evenings, half price. 151 Third St. at Howard St. (phone: 357-4000).

Wells Fargo History Museum The history room features Old California, with photographs and relics from the Gold Rush days, including the *Wells Fargo Overland Stage* (the wagon that brought pioneers west) as well as coins, placers, and hard rock gold from mother lode mines. Closed weekends. No admission charge. 420 Montgomery St. (phone: 396-2619).

Other museums worth a visit include the following:

AFRICAN-AMERICAN HISTORICAL AND CULTURAL SOCIETY A museum and library honoring black history and culture. Open Wednesdays through Sundays, afternoons only. Admission charge. *Fort Mason,* Bldg. C (phone: 441-0640).

ANSEL ADAMS CENTER Changing exhibitions are devoted to the extraordinary photographs of this San Francisco native and environmentalist and to the works of other great photographers. Closed Mondays. Admission charge. 250 Fourth St. (phone: 495-7000).

BAY AREA DISCOVERY MUSEUM Housed in the historic buildings of *Fort Baker* in Marin County, this "please touch" museum is geared to children two to 12, but is interesting for anyone with a "let me try" attitude. The *Architecture and Design Building* is equipped with drafting tables and tools, PVC tubes for large-scale construction, and a contractor's corner for art projects. In the *San Francisco Bay Exhibit* a fishing vessel rocks in an imaginary sea as youngsters reel in salmon and other deep-sea fish. A crawl-through underwater tunnel provides a fish-eye view of animal and plant life. Older explorers can rent backpacks filled with containers, nets, a hand lens, and eye dropper (along with guides to fish and intertidal life) to examine the "bay soup" just steps away in Horseshoe Cove. Closed Mondays, and on Tuesdays from *Labor Day* to *Memorial Day.* Admission charge. 557 E. Ft. Baker Rd. (first exit on Highway 101 north, just over the *Golden Gate Bridge;* phone: 332-7674).

CABLE CAR MUSEUM Served by the two Powell Street cable car lines, this small museum celebrates and explains the mysterious workings of one of the city's great treasures and attractions. As it overlooks the powerhouse, visitors can watch great wheels pull the cables at a steady 9.5 mph. A 15-minute film gives an explanation of how the cars work. No. 8, the first cable car operated by Andrew Hallidie, who inaugurated the system on Clay Street in 1873, sits on a pedestal. A gift shop offers a wide selection of souvenirs and memorabilia. Open daily. No admission charge. 1201 Mason St. (phone: 474-1887).

CALIFORNIA ACADEMY OF SCIENCE Everything new (and old, this being the first scientific institution to have been founded in California) under the sun is at the *California Academy of Science,* actually three interconnected museums housed under one roof. The *Steinhart Aquarium* is home to thousands of fish, amphibians, and marine mammals. Dolphins and seals are friskiest and most fun to watch at feeding times (10:30 AM; 12:30, 2:30, and 4:30 PM), although they never seem to tire of company. The "fish roundabout" provides the current needed for large species of shark and cod. At the tide-pool the non-squeamish can pick up, poke, and even sniff the starfish, hermit crabs, and other sea life usually visible only at ebb tide. "Life Through Time: The Evidence for Evolution" is the large exhibit in the *Natural History Museum,* which also features realistic displays on wildlife environments, anthropology, and gems and minerals. The *Morrison Planetarium* delves into the mysteries of Earth and space; sky-show laser performances are scheduled regularly at the *Laserium.* One of the most popular exhibits is the "SafeQuake," a platform that simulates the ground movement of two different earthquakes, while a short video shows footage of the real thing. Open daily *July 4* through *Labor Day.* Admission charge. *Music Concourse, Golden Gate Park* (phone: 221-5100).

CARTOON ART MUSEUM Exhibited here are original editorial, newspaper, and magazine cartoons, various animation boards, plus five 1789 works by British artist William Hogarth, considered to be among the first cartoons ever created. Special events include lectures and Saturday conversations with cartoonists (call the hotline at 546-9481 for schedules). Closed Sundays through Tuesdays. Admission charge. 665 Third St., Fifth Floor (phone: 546-3922).

CRAFT AND FOLK ART MUSEUM This museum houses changing, lively exhibitions of contemporary crafts and folk art. It also has a small shop. Closed Mondays and Tuesdays. Admission charge. *Fort Mason,* Bldg. A (phone: 775-0990).

EXPLORATORIUM Expect to hear such sophisticated reactions as "wow" and "cool" when visiting the *Exploratorium.* Touching is a "must" here—more than 650 exhibits require pushing, pulling, throwing, or some other participation to explore the forces of the physical world. Light, sound, gravity, and perception are just four of the subjects examined. The *Tactile Dome*—a definite favorite among the small set—is a touchy-feely experience; crawl through a series of pitch-black tunnels, using your sense of touch to guide you. (Because of its popularity, advance reservations are required for the *Tactile Dome,* but there is no additional admission charge.) Closed Mondays. Admission charge. 3601 Lyon St. (inside the *Palace of Fine Arts*; phone: 561-0360 for recorded information; 561-0362 for *Tactile Dome* reservations).

JEWISH MUSEUM OF SAN FRANCISCO Devoted to a lively exploration of Jewish traditions and art as they relate to current affairs, the galleries and shop are open Sundays through Thursdays, with a 7 PM closing on Thursday; closed holidays. Admission charge. 121 Steuart St., near the Embarcadero *BART* station (phone: 543-8880).

MEXICAN MUSEUM Colorful displays of handicrafts and paintings from south-of-the-border artists. Closed Mondays and Tuesdays. Admission charge. *Fort Mason*, Bldg. D (phone: 441-0404).

MUSEUM OF THE CITY OF SAN FRANCISCO Rotating art exhibits depict the wide diversity of this city by the bay and the struggles of its people. Closed Mondays and Tuesdays. No admission charge. *The Cannery*, 2801 Leavenworth (phone: 928-0289).

RANDALL JUNIOR MUSEUM Another hands-on experience, with the emphasis here on art and nature. In the live animal room, visitors can get close to more than 50 different species, including rabbits, hawks, and owls. Those bold enough can explore the museum's collection of spiders, snakes, and insects. An elaborate exhibit of working toy trains is open on the second and fourth Saturdays of the month. Children can learn about dinosaurs and minerals, and can explore ceramics and woodworking in the classes offered here. If that's not enough, a seismograph tracks earthquakes around the world. Situated atop a 16-acre hill near Twin Peaks, the museum also offers a beautiful view of the city. Closed Sundays and Mondays. No admission charge. 199 Museum Way (phone: 554-9600).

SAN FRANCISCO ART COMMISSION GALLERY Emerging Bay Area artists exhibit paintings, sculpture, and nontraditional art forms. Open Thursday through Saturday, afternoons only (Thursday until 8). No admission charge. 155 Grove St. (phone: 554-9682).

SAN FRANCISCO PERFORMING ARTS LIBRARY AND MUSEUM Displays and an extensive research collection of posters, programs, reviews, and other memorabilia. Closed Sundays and Mondays. No admission charge. 399 Grove St., near the *Civic Center* (phone: 255-4800).

MAJOR COLLEGES AND UNIVERSITIES

Two of the country's most prestigious universities are near San Francisco: the *University of California at Berkeley* (phone: 510-642-6000) and *Stanford University* in Palo Alto (phone: 723-2300). *San Francisco State University* (1600 Holloway Ave.; phone: 338-1111); the Jesuit-run *University of San Francisco* (Golden Gate and Parker Aves.; phone: 666-6886); and the *UCSF Medical Center* (505 Parnassus Ave.; phone: 476-1000) are located within the city limits.

SHOPPING

In the various neighborhoods as well as downtown, shopping is easy in this relatively compact city. For Japanese wares one can go to Japantown; for Chinese, Chinatown. With *Ghirardelli Square, The Cannery*, the *Anchorage* on *Fisherman's Wharf*, and *Pier 39*, San Francisco revived the age-old combination of marketplace and fun fair. *Embarcadero Center*, between the waterfront and the financial district, is filled with shops and restaurants. *San Francisco Centre*, on Market Street near Powell Street, is a stunning, polished-stone structure with a huge, retractable skylight and spiral escalators; *Nordstrom* is the anchor department store here. The highly decorative *Rincon Center,* on Mission Street between Main and Spear Streets, was once an Art Deco–style post office; it now has a restored lobby, a 90-foot waterfall, 30 shops, and several good restaurants. When serious buying is the object—and money is not—the place to be is Union Square and the streets that frame it. On the square are four major department stores: *Macy's, Saks Fifth Avenue, I. Magnin,* and *Neiman Marcus.* Nearby specialty shops include firms from Britain, France, Germany, Italy, and Switzerland plus US competitors. Not to be confused with Union Square is a shopping stretch of Union Street on the old dairy land, Cow Hollow, and another on Fillmore Street. Victorian Union Street has exotic and unusual gift shops and designer boutiques featuring European fashions, while Fillmore's specialty is new and vintage fashion and home furnishings. For bargains in high fashion, explore the factory outlets south of Market Street (SoMa). A number of discount stores have opened up in this area; clothing prices are great, but shop decor is usually threadbare. Here's a window shopper's view of the famous, the classic, and the unusual:

UNION SQUARE

Dorothy Weiss Gallery Ceramic sculptures are the stock in trade at this upscale gallery two blocks east of Union Square. 256 Sutter St. (phone: 397-3611).

Giants Dugout Store Paraphernalia for followers of the orange and black and other sports teams; ticket sales, too. 170 Grant Ave. (phone: 982-9400).

Gump's Famous for its jade, art, jewelry, crystal, china, sculpture, furniture, antiques, stationery, and food. 250 Post St. (phone: 982-1616).

Jean-Marc Big, bold designs and colors in women's wear. 262 Sutter St. (phone: 362-1121).

Jessica McClintock Original beaded, lacy fashions for women and girls. 353 Sutter St. (phone: 397-0987).

Obiko One-of-a-kind women's clothing with an artistic bent by contemporary designers. 794 Sutter St. (phone: 775-2882).

La Parisienne Fine jewelry designed and made in Paris, as well as genuine French lithographs, all well priced. 460 Post St. (phone: 788-2255).

Shreve & Co. One of San Francisco's oldest purveyors of the finest silver, crystal, and jewelry. 200 Post St. (phone: 421-2600).

Sidney Mobell Anything and everything that can possibly be studded with jewels, including yo-yos, Frisbees, and fax machines. 950 Mason St. (in the *Fairmont* hotel; phone: 986-4747 or 800-442-7999).

Smile Truly "tongue in chic": arts and crafts with a sense of humor. 500 Sutter St. (phone: 362-3436).

Wilkes Bashford High-priced men's and women's clothing. 375 Sutter St. (phone: 986-4380).

HAYES STREET

Antonio Conti Handmade, one-of-a-kind furniture from Bay Area craftspeople. 416 Hayes St. (phone: 864-8307).

Country Java Teak furniture, including pieces that the owner, Terry Starke, shipped from his own home in Java. 572 Hayes St. (phone: 552-2767).

Evelyn's The best collection of Chinese antiques in the city. Head back to the warehouse to see its floor-to-ceiling collection. 381 Hayes St. (phone: 255-1815).

F. Dorian, Inc. Hand-crafted collectibles of many cultures, including Mexican, African, and Asian. 388 Hayes St. (phone: 861-3191).

Richard Hilkert Books Books on art, music, design, and architecture. 333 Hayes St. (phone 863-3339).

de Vera Italian and Swedish glass from the 1950s and 1960s along with stunning art glass collected by Federico de Vera. 384 Hayes St. (phone: 861-8480).

Victorian Interiors Everything necessary from decorative wall moldings to brass bath fixtures to spiff up (or create) your Victorian-era dream home. 575 Hayes St. (phone: 431-7191).

Zonal Metal and other materials are fashioned into unique sculptures and other artworks. 568 Hayes St. (phone: 255-9307).

MID-MARKET

Bell'occhio A unique and whimsical collection of dried flowers, antique and hand-dyed ribbons, unusual soaps, sachets, and eccentric little boxes. 8 Brady St. (phone: 864-4048).

Decorum Art Deco furnishings. 1632 Market St. (phone: 864-3326).

Red Desert A wide range of cacti and succulent plants, which can be shipped throughout the country, and other finds from the desert. 1632 Market St. (phone: 552-2800).

20th Century Furniture American pieces made from 1930 to 1960. 1612 Market St. (phone: 626-0542).

UNION STREET

Bauer Antiques Mostly French treasures. 1878 Union St. (phone: 921-7656).

Carnevale An eclectic assortment of dresses and hats by American designers. 2206 Union St. (phone: 931-0669).

Coco's Italian Dream Romantic-looking satin and lace women's clothing. 2254 Union St. (phone: 346-9986).

Dolls and Bears of Charlton Court Antique and collectors' one-of-a-kind dolls and teddy bears. 1957 Union St. (phone: 775-3740).

John Wheatman & Assoc. English- and Japanese-style antique and contemporary furniture. 1933 Union St. (phone: 346-8300).

Oggetti Marbleized Florentine papers sold by the sheet, or used on picture frames or to cover treasure boxes and photo albums. Other gift items, too. 1846 Union St. (phone: 346-0631).

Paris 1925 Antique watches and Art Deco jewelry. 1954 Union St., Second Floor (phone: 567-1925).

Sy Aal High-style men's fashions designed from a woman's point of view. 1864 Union St. (phone: 929-1864).

Three Bags Full Fabulous sweaters hand-knit with luxurious yarns. 2181 Union St. (phone: 567-5753).

Uko Japanese fashions for men, women, and children. 2070 Union St. (phone: 563-0330).

Yankee Doodle Dandy Cute country crafts and handmade quilts. 1974 Union St. (phone: 346-0346).

Zuni Pueblo A tribe-owned store featuring contemporary Zuni arts. 1749 Union St. (phone: 567-0941).

FILLMORE STREET

Cedanna Arts and crafts by Northern California artists, as well as pottery, a selection of fine foods, and interesting housewares. 1925 Fillmore St. (phone: 474-7152).

Zoe Far-out, expensive women's clothes. 2400 Fillmore St. (phone: 929-0441).

OUTER SACRAMENTO STREET

Dandelion A browser's paradise filled with books, boxes, glassware, gardening tools, and a little bit of everything else. Perhaps the city's best gift shop. 2877 California St. at Broderick St. (phone: 563-3100).

Forrest Jones Everything you might need for the well-accessorized kitchen and dining table. 3274 Sacramento St. (phone 567-2483).

Jasper Byron French and English antiques, reproductions, and accessories in the classic style. 3364 Sacramento St. (phone: 563-8122).

The Master's Mark Custom-designed, custom-built furniture adapted from traditional Asian styles. 3228 Sacramento St. (phone: 885-6700).

Santa Fe Handwoven Mexican blankets and color-faded furniture in the Southwestern style. 3571 Sacramento St. (phone: 346-0180).

Sue Fisher King Elegant linen and accessories for bed and table. 3067 Sacramento St. (phone: 922-7276).

V. Breier Contemporary and traditional crafts, including neon sculpture and colorful ceramics, imaginative jewelry and furniture, and baskets made of handmade papers, leaves, pine cones, and seed pods. 3091 Sacramento St. (phone: 929-7173).

Walker-McIntyre Antiques Exquisite 18th- and 19th-century English furnishings along with Chinese and Japanese accessories. 3419 Sacramento St. (phone: 563-8024).

SOUTH OF MARKET STREET (SOMA)

Baker Hamilton Square A dozen shops selling antiques, art, and furnishings share space in a historic warehouse. Near the train station at Seventh and Townsend Sts. (phone: 861-3500).

Basic Brown Bears At this teddy bear lair you can watch the cuddly creatures being made, then pick out one who's ready to travel. 444 De Haro St. (phone: 626-0781).

Discount Bridal Brides-to-be travel cross-country for wedding dresses at sensational savings. 300 Brannon St. (phone: 495-7922).

Esprit An outlet branch of the popular sportswear company; there's also a great café. 499 Illinois St. (phone: 957-2550).

LIMN Company Avant-garde art and furniture. 290 Townsend St. (phone: 543-5466).

Six Sixty Center Twenty discount outlets under one roof selling everything from sweaters and jeans to jewelry and cosmetics. 660 Third St. (phone: 227-0464).

FOR BOOKWORMS

San Francisco is rich in literary history, having been home to such diverse writers as Jack London and Jack Kerouac. Others whose creative juices flowed here include Mark Twain, Robert Louis Stevenson, Dashiell Hammett, and Amy Tan. Below are some of San Francisco's favorite reading rooms.

City Lights Launched by Beat poet Lawrence Ferlinghetti in 1953, this landmark bookstore was the first to sell paperbacks only. Hardcover books eventually found space here as well, and the shelves are lined with hard-to-find and esoteric titles. In addition to an excellent selection of contemporary poetry, this bookstore offers an unusual selection of Third World literature and volumes on literary and language theory. Though it has grown to be much more, this is still the place to come for the works of Beat writers. The staff is an eclectic and knowledgeable bunch, and each decides what to order within his or her special field of expertise. 261 Columbus Ave. (phone: 362-8193).

A Clean, Well Lighted Place for Books Borrowing its name from an Ernest Hemingway short story, this is San Francisco's largest independent bookstore. As its name suggests, it is clean and well lit. More important, it offers an impressive selection of books with particularly strong fiction, science fiction, mystery, and music sections. Its location makes it a perfect place to stop before or after the symphony, opera, or ballet. Two book signings and readings, by either national or local authors, usually are scheduled each week. It's worth a call to see who will be there, as this can be stimulating, inexpensive entertainment. 601 Van Ness Ave., near the *Civic Center* (phone: 441-6670).

McDonald's "A dirty, poorly lit place for books" is how this shop describes itself—a play on the well-known bookstore described above. This is the largest used bookstore in town; the owners claim an inventory of more than a million books, records, and magazines. Things are packed, piled, stacked, and some even make their way onto shelves. Put aside some time to browse here. If you're looking for something out of print, there's a good chance *McDonald's* has it—or can tell you where to find it. Among the store's offerings are back issues of *TV Guide*—which they say they stock for people with old TV sets. No credit cards accepted. 48 Turk St. (phone: 673-2235).

Serious book browsers should also consider crossing the bay to the bookstores of Berkeley, where waiters have master's degrees and auto mechanics have PhDs, the bookstores reflect that. Look for *Cody's Books* (phone: 510-845-7852) and *Moe*'s (phone: 510-849-2087), both on Telegraph Avenue, and *Black Oak Books* on Shattuck Avenue (phone: 510-486-0698).

SPORTS AND FITNESS

Any successful local professional team plays to a full house, especially the *Giants* (their fans are awarded an icicle-draped "Croix de Candlestick" pin for surviving an extra-inning night game in windy *Candlestick Park*). However, mild year-round weather and varied terrain lures bikers, boaters, and joggers away from arenas, stadiums, and TV sets.

BASEBALL The San Francisco Giants play from April to October in Candlestick Park (Gilman Ave., on the southern edge of the city east of US 101; phone: 467-8000). The Oakland A's play at the Oakland Coliseum (7000 Coliseum Way; phone: 510-638-4900).

BASKETBALL The NBA's *Golden State Warriors* play from October to April at the *Oakland Coliseum Arena* (phone: 510-638-6300 for information; 510-762-BASS for tickets).

BICYCLING A general tour of San Francisco on a bicycle is not the safest way to see the sights, but there are some fine routes that offer grand views with less risk. Mountain bikes can be rented from *Magic Skates and Bikes* at *Golden Gate Park* (3038 Fulton St. at Sixth Ave.; phone: 668-1117). Pedaling along the city's scenic shoreline is breathtaking, even if you don't attempt the hills. On Sundays, roads through the middle of *Golden Gate Park* are off limits to automobiles, which provides a respite from the treachery of riding side by side with cars. Another favorite route is past the Presidio and over the *Golden Gate Bridge.* More ambitious riders head to Sausalito or through the (very hilly) Marin Headlands to the beaches of Marin County. Bike route maps are available at most bicycle shops.

FISHING For anglers there is a top fishing spot right in the city; there's also fine salmon fishing in the sea beyond the bay.

BEST BITE

Lake Merced At the southern end of the city, near the shoreline, Lake Merced is actually two lakes running along the San Andreas Fault. Fed by freshwater springs, the dunes of *Fort Funston* keep the water from flowing into the ocean. Both lakes, which plummet to depths of 30 feet, are stocked with trout every week. A California fishing permit and a daily use permit are required; rods and reels can be rented from *Lake Merced Boating and Fishing* (phone: 753-1101). Rowboats, sailboats, canoes, motorboats, and pedalboats can also be rented at the lake. In addition to the ducks and swans that paddle along the marshy shores, bird watchers will find loons, grebes, and other waterfowl. The lake is located at 1 Harding Road off Skyline Boulevard, near the *San Francisco Zoo.*

For those who have good sea legs, the trip under the *Golden Gate Bridge* and out into the Pacific is an exhilarating experience. Salmon season runs from March to mid-October. Charter boats leave daily early in the morning and return in the afternoon. *New Easy Rider Sport Fishing* (phone: 285-2000) is based at the *Berkeley Marina,* and *Wacky Jacky* (phone: 586-9800) sails from *Fisherman's Wharf* at *Pier 39.* You also can cast off San Francisco's municipal pier at *Aquatic Park* anytime (also see *San Francisco Maritime National Historic Park* in *Special Places,* above). No license required.

FITNESS CENTERS *Fitness Break* (30 Hotaling Pl. near Washington and Montgomery Sts.; phone: 788-1681) offers weekday workouts; showers and lockers are available. The *YMCA* (169 Steuart St.; phone: 957-9622) has a pool, sauna, and weight room (including Nautilus, Cybex, and cardiovascular exercise equipment), along with racquetball and handball courts and aerobics classes.

FOOTBALL The San Francisco *49ers* play from August to December (and sometimes even in January) at *Candlestick Park* (Gilman Ave., on the southern edge of the city east of US 101; phone: 468-2249).

GOLF Serious golfers may find it difficult to resist the temptation of driving down the coast about two hours to the world class courses on the Monterey Peninsula. For those who don't mind a wee-hours-in-the-morning wake-up call, we've listed the *Pebble Beach* links below. For those who would rather stay near the city, there are good public golf courses right in the Bay Area.

A TOP TEE-OFF SPOT

Pebble Beach Golf Links If there is a leading contender for the title of Most Photographed Golf Course, it has to be the ocean-hugging *Pebble Beach Golf Links* on the windswept Monterey Peninsula. This is one of the rare cases of a truly first class US tournament track being occasionally accessible to the public: Reservations are open one day in advance and are based on cancellations, which are rare. However, guests at the *Lodge at Pebble Beach* (phone: 408-624-3811) and the *Inn at Spanish Bay* (phone: 408-647-7500) have unrestricted use of this sought-after course. Seventeen Mile Dr., Pebble Beach, CA 93953 (phone: 800-654-9300 for tee-time reservations).

Just 1 mile from *Pebble Beach Golf Links,* and considered so difficult that even the touring pros complain about it, is *Spyglass Hill* (Stevenson Dr., Pebble Beach, CA 93953; phone: 800-654-9300). This 18-hole beauty was designed by Robert Trent Jones Sr. and is the home course for the *Pebble Beach Ben Hogan Invitational* (for both the PGA and LPGA).

San Francisco boasts fine public courses at *Lincoln Park* (34th Ave. and Clement St.; phone: 221-9911) and *Harding Park* (Skyline Blvd. and Harding Rd.; phone: 664-4690).

HOCKEY The NHL's *San Jose Sharks* play at the 18,000-seat *Downtown Arena,* on The Alameda near Guadalupe Pkwy. (phone: 800-BE-SHARK for ticket information).

HORSE RACING *Bay Meadows* is the place, in San Mateo (phone: 574-7223). The season begins in August and runs into January. In the East Bay *Golden Gate Fields* features thoroughbred racing from late February through late June (phone: 510-559-7300).

HORSEBACK RIDING Guided trail rides and lessons are available at *Golden Gate Stables* at *Golden Gate Park* (John F. Kennedy Dr. at 36th Ave.; phone:

668-7360). Twelve miles of bridle paths wind through the park. Reservations necessary.

JOGGING Run from the *Ferry Building* along *The Embarcadero* to *Fort Point* beneath the *Golden Gate Bridge* (6 miles one way); jog back and forth across the *Golden Gate Bridge* (1½ miles each way) and enjoy the fore and aft views, as well as the one directly below. From Market Street via the *Civic Center* the 21 Hayes bus goes to *Golden Gate Park,* where there are numerous dirt and concrete trails, not to mention plenty of other joggers. (Do not run alone in secluded areas of the park.)

SKATING Roller-skating is very popular in San Francisco, especially in *Golden Gate Park* on Sundays, when traffic is detoured off the park's main roads. You can rent skates from *Magic Skates* (3038 Fulton St. at Sixth Ave.; phone: 668-1117), right across from the park.

SWIMMING Though much of San Francisco's waters are too rough and cold for swimming, Phelan Beach (at Sea Cliff Ave. and El Camino del Mar) is good when the weather permits and the current is safe. The *Sheehan* hotel pool and work-out area (620 Sutter St.; phone: 775-6500) is open to the public daily.

TENNIS The *San Francisco Recreation and Parks Department* (phone: 666-7200) maintains more than a hundred tennis courts around the city. Free to the public, they are available on a first-come, first-served basis. *Golden Gate Park* has 21 courts, which can be reserved in advance on weekends for a nominal fee. *Golden Gate Park* at *McLaren Lodge* (Fell and Stanyan Sts.; phone: 753-7101).

YACHT RACING The *Yacht Racing Association* holds most of its races between April and mid-October, but mid-winter regattas also are held. Races start and end off the *Marina Green* and turn at Blossom Rock Buoy beyond *Pier 39* (phone: 771-9500 for information).

THEATER

The *American Conservatory Theater* is an excellent resident repertory company, which performs classical productions and modern plays from October to June. Temporarily turned out of its home at the *Geary Theater* because of 1989 earthquake damage, it is scheduled to reopen this year. While the company makes repairs it performs at other local theaters: the *Stage Door* (420 Mason St.) and the *Orpheum* (1192 Market St. at Hyde St.); for tickets, contact the *ACT* Box Office (415 Geary St., San Francisco, CA 94102; phone: 749-2200). The *Curran Theater* is a venue for musicals and often stages traveling Broadway productions (445 Geary St.; phone: 474-3800). The *Orpheum Theater* (1192 Market St.; phone: 474-3800) and the *Golden Gate Theater* (Golden Gate and Taylor Sts.; phone: 474-3800) also feature Broadway shows. *Shakespeare in the Park* is performed free from *Labor Day* through October in *Liberty Tree Meadow* behind the conservatory in *Golden*

Gate Park (phone: 666-2221). At *Club Fugazi,* an old North Beach land-mark, the camp cult classic *Beach Blanket Babylon* (see *San Franciso's Sounds of Music* in DIVERSIONS) has been running for 18 years (678 Green St.; phone: 421-4222). If you have an urge to see the world through cellu-loid, visit the *Castro,* a 1922 landmark theater—complete with an organ-ist—that shows classic films (Castro St. near Market St.; phone: 621-6120). Or try the *Paramount,* which holds four Friday night classic film series, including newsreels, cartoons, vintage trailers, and spin-the-wheel door prizes. The theater itself is a prize; tours are offered on the first and third Saturdays of the month at 10 AM. Meticulously maintained, this Art Deco building is in the *National Register of Historic Places* (2025 Broadway, near the 19th St. *BART* station in Oakland; phone: 510-465-6400). The *San Francisco Ballet,* the country's oldest company and among its finest, moves into the *War Memorial Opera House* in the *Civic Center* with its *Nutcracker* production in December, followed by a repertory season from January through May (Van Ness Ave. and Grove St.; phone: 703-9400).

MUSIC

The *San Francisco Opera Association* is a world class opera company. It per-forms at the *War Memorial Opera House* (*Civic Center;* phone: 864-3330) from September to early December; the summer season is May and early June. Since tickets are difficult to get, it's best to reserve in advance (*War Memorial Opera House* Box Office, San Francisco, CA 94102). The *San Francisco Symphony* season runs from September through May at *Louise M. Davies Symphony Hall* in the *Civic Center* (phone: 431-5400), but the orchestra can be heard at other times, too, such as during its *June Beethoven Festival* or its July *Pops Concerts* in the *Civic Auditorium.* The *Midsummer Music Festival* is a free Sunday series of symphony, opera, jazz, and ethnic programs from mid-June to mid-August at *Sigmund Stern Grove* (19th Ave. and Sloat Blvd.; phone: 252-6252). See also *San Francisco's Sounds of Music* in DIVERSIONS.

Tickets for most music, dance, and theater events can be obtained through *BASS* ticket centers (phone: 510-762-BASS). In addition, half-price as well as full-price tickets to many events can be bought (cash or traveler's checks only) on the day of performance at the *TIX* booth on the Stockton Street side of Union Square, Tuesdays through Saturdays from 11 AM to 7:30 PM (phone: 433-7827; you must go to the booth for information on half-price tickets).

NIGHTCLUBS AND NIGHTLIFE

San Francisco is alive at night and can keep you going whether you're inclined toward jazz, pop, or alternative rock. The nightlife glitters all around the city. Current favorites: the *Great American Music Hall* (859 O'Farrell St.; phone: 885-0750), for major jazz and folk artists, and *Lascaux* (248 Sutter St.; phone: 391-1555), for jazz. For comedy: *Cobb's Comedy Club* (2801 Leavenworth St., in *The Cannery;* phone: 928-4320) and *Punch Line*

(444 Battery St.; phone: 397-7573). For cabaret try the *Plush Room* (940 Sutter St.; phone: 885-2800). For a view of San Francisco at night try the *Top of the Mark* in the *Mark Hopkins Inter-Continental* hotel; *Oz,* a nightclub atop the *Westin St. Francis* hotel (see *Checking In* for both); or the *Starlite Roof* in the *Sir Francis Drake* hotel (Powell St. at Sutter St.; phone: 392-7755). Dance to the Brazilian beat at *Bahia Tropical* (1600 Market St. at Franklin St.; phone: 861-8657) or to rhythm and blues at *Harry Denton's* (161 Steuart St.; phone: 882-1333). The younger crowd heads to SoMa—the district south of Market Street. On Fridays the nightclub at 1015 Folsom Street (phone: 431-1200) is dubbed *Martini,* featuring diverse music and hetero clubgoers; Saturday nights its name changes to *Product,* which caters to a lively gay crowd. On lower Haight *Nickies* (460 Haight St.; phone: 621-6508) is popular—one night the music is hip-hop, the next it's salsa. The *Elbo Room* (647 Valencia St.; phone: 552-7788) has a hip crowd, with live music upstairs. *Johnny Love's* (1500 Broadway at Polk; phone 931-6053) appeals to a wide range of tastes with offerings of R&B, jazz, American rock, world beat, and reggae. In addition, the historic *Fillmore* (1805 Geary St., near Japantown; phone: 346-6000 for recorded information) reopened last year as a restaurant, bar, and performance hall. Tickets to performances can be purchased at *BASS* outlets (phone: 510-762-BASS).

Be warned that San Francisco's red-light district, not particularly garish by day, roars to life at night in the Tenderloin, an area near the theater district; centered between Union Square and the *Civic Center,* it is bordered by Jones Street, O'Farrell Street, Polk Street, and Golden Gate Avenue. While sleazy, the area is not an absolute no-go zone, although one theater, the *Golden Gate,* is on a block where the prostitutes are particularly aggressive.

Best in Town

CHECKING IN

President Taft called San Francisco "the town that knows how," and though he probably wasn't talking about hotels, his statement nonetheless applies. A pleasant embarrassment of riches confronts visitors, from luxurious mammoths to ritzy mid-size establishments to dozens of intimate "boutique" hotels, which mimic European small hotels in character. Expect to pay over $200 per night for a double room in the very expensive bracket; $140 to $200, expensive; $80 to $140, moderate; and under $80, inexpensive. Most of San Francisco's major hotels have complete facilities for the business traveler. Those hotels listed below as having "business services" usually offer such conveniences as an English-speaking concierge, meeting rooms, photocopiers, computers, translation services, and express checkout, among others. Call the hotel for additional information. All telephone numbers are in the 415 area code unless otherwise indicated.

For bed and breakfast lodgings contact *American Family Inn/Bed & Breakfast San Francisco* (PO Box 420009, San Francisco, CA 94142; phone: 931-3083); or *Bed & Breakfast International* (PO Box 282910, San Francisco, CA 94128-2910; phone: 696-1690 or 800-272-4500; fax: 696-1699) for special accommodations (in a houseboat, aboard a yacht, or even in a Victorian mansion). For daily, weekly, or monthly rentals of condominiums, townhouses, apartments, and homes, contact *American Property Exchange* (170 Page St., San Francisco, CA 94102; phone: 863-8484). Always ask about special packages and discounts.

For an unforgettable experience in San Francisco, we begin with our favorites, followed by our cost and quality choices of accommodations, listed by price category.

GRAND HOTELS AND SPECIAL HAVENS

Archbishop's Mansion Inn This stately structure built in 1904 once served as the home of San Francisco's Archbishop Riordon. Now a romantic bed and breakfast establishment, all of its 15 rooms (all named for operas) have fireplaces and private baths. Antiques and Oriental carpets grace the rooms; fine embroidered linen dresses the beds. Breakfast is delivered to your door each morning, and complimentary wine is served in the parlor every evening. Business services are available. 1000 Fulton St. (phone: 563-7872 or 800-543-5820; fax: 885-3193).

Fairmont Old World charm still reigns supreme here, although the lavish lobby has become a bit tattered with all the wear and tear. Gawkers often crowd in to see its dark wood paneling, gold-leaf moldings, and deep-red upholstered sofas. Originally scheduled to open in 1906, the massive, Italian Renaissance–style building withstood the great earthquake but was gutted by fire; a year later it had a triumphant opening with a party that celebrated the city's rebirth. There are 596 rooms and eight restaurants and cocktail lounges (with two orchestras). In the tower section rooms facing north and west afford views of the fog rolling in under the *Golden Gate Bridge*. A luxurious three-bedroom penthouse suite (renting for $6,000 a night!) boasts a patio, a fireplace with lapis lazuli inlays, and a gold-leaf depiction of the constellations on the library's domed ceiling. In 1945 Secretary of State Edward Stettinius drafted the United Nations charter in this opulent setting. The health club and twice-daily maid service add to the experience. Business services are available. 950 Mason St. (phone: 772-5000 or 800-527-4727; fax: 781-3929).

Four Seasons Clift The warmth of rich wood paneling is matched by the warm, personalized service of the staff at this refined, 329-room property. Some of its employees have been on staff long enough to serve return guests for decades. Attention to detail can be seen in every corner—each room is individually decorated, and even at 2 AM room service can deliver a perfect cheeseburger in 20 minutes. The antiques-filled lobby harkens to another, more gracious time, and a Viennese dessert buffet is served in the *French Room* in the late evening until midnight. Built from a single giant sequoia, the *Redwood Room* has an altogether different ambience; its selection of cognacs and ports is one of the city's best. The hotel's "Very Important Kids" program pampers children and teens. Playtime offerings include computer and board games, books, toys, and a VCR and tape library. Located next door to the *Curran Theatre,* the hotel offers theatergoer packages. Business services are available. 495 Geary St. (phone: 775-4700 or 800-332-3442; fax: 441-4621).

Huntington The gold-and-burgundy antiques-filled lobby exudes elegance in this former apartment building. Each of its 140 spacious rooms is distinctively decorated and comfortable, and many have outstanding views. Upon arrival you are welcomed with sherry or a formal tea. The *Big Four* restaurant (the name refers to four railroad millionaires) looks like a turn-of-the-century men's club and serves fish, chops, and steaks. Guest privileges also include use of the exclusive *Nob Hill Health Club* on the next block, and a sleek, chauffeured Lincoln Town Car provides complimentary transportation within downtown. Business services are available. 1075 California St. (phone: 474-5400; 800-652-1539 in California; 800-227-4683 elsewhere in the US; fax: 474-6227).

Inn at the Opera This small (and reasonably priced), European-style, 48-room hostelry affords easy access to the culturally rich *Civic Center* area, which has improved since the demolition of the nearby elevated freeway. International luminaries like Mikhail Baryshnikov and Luciano Pavarotti stay here, sleeping in small but luxurious rooms with canopy beds, fresh-cut flowers, kitchenettes with microwave ovens, and mini-bars. Pre- and post-performance dinners and desserts are served in the inn's English-inspired, fireplace-cozy *Act IV* restaurant. Promotional packages with tickets to the symphony, opera, and ballet are occasionally offered. Business services are available, there's a concierge on duty 24 hours a day, and free limousine service to downtown is provided weekdays. 333 Fulton St. (phone: 863-8400; 800-423-9610 in California; 800-325-2708 elsewhere in the US; fax: 861-0821).

Ritz-Carlton Another of the city's historic landmarks, this grand neo-classical structure was completed in 1909. It was first home to the Metropolitan Life Insurance Company, then to *Cogswell College*. After total interior renovations lasting four years, the building was reopened in 1991 as the *Ritz*. Its wholly preserved, early-20th-century exterior, tastefully elegant decor, and high level of service make it worthy of its Nob Hill address. The lobby and guestrooms are filled with antiques and 18th-century artwork; only the fitness center and indoor pool are modern. There are 336 guestrooms and 44 suites, two restaurants, including the elegant *Dining Room,* two lounges, and a courtyard, where jazz brunches are held from May to October. Business services are available. Between Nob Hill and the financial district at California and Stockton Sts. (phone: 296-7465 or 800-241-3333; fax: 291-0288).

Sheraton Palace When the *Palace* hotel opened its doors in 1875, it was the largest and most luxurious hotel in the world. With the completion of a massive renovation, this landmark hostelry regained its Old World atmosphere while adding many modern-day touches, such as a spa with an indoor lap pool, whirlpool bath, and sauna; all manner of business amenities are offered. Returned to its former glory, the hotel exudes sophisticated elegance; all 550 guestrooms (with marble bathrooms and antique furnishings) and even the elegant *Garden Court*—where massive Italian marble columns support a domed ceiling of iridescent glass—are reminiscent of a 19th-century mansion. It's here that the old guard present their daughters at the annual cotillion. A Maxfield Parrish mural, *The Pied Piper of Hamlin,* hangs in the *Pied Piper Bar*. Nonsmoking floors and handicapped-accessible rooms are available. 2 New Montgomery St., adjacent to the financial district (phone: 392-8600 or 800-325-3535; fax: 543-0671).

Sherman House Once the private mansion of music store owner Leander Sherman, this 14-room inn is the only San Francisco member of the prestigious international Relais & Châteaux group. Interior designer Billy Gaylord created the decor, featuring French Second Empire and Biedermeier design elements. Guestrooms are furnished with handwoven Persian carpets, fireplaces, feather beds, and down comforters. Some suites have terraces that afford a view of the *Golden Gate Bridge*. Built in 1876 in the Victorian Italianate style, it has a three-story music room where Sherman used to entertain his famous guests (among them, Lillian Russell and Enrico Caruso). French-inspired food is served in the simply named *Dining Room;* room service is available around the clock. 2160 Green St. (phone: 563-3600 or 800-424-5777; fax: 563-1882).

Stouffer–Stanford Court Set back from the street, the entryway of this 402-room hostelry includes a Beaux Arts fountain and Tiffany-style glass dome. Built on the site of 19th-century Governor Leland Stanford's mansion, this property is now a link in the Stouffer hotel chain. A stay here can include coffee and the newspaper with your wake-up call, afternoon tea and/or wine in the lobby bar, dinner in the hotel's *Fournou's Oven*—and a Rolls-Royce Phantom VI limousine to whisk you off to the theater. No details are overlooked: Breads are baked fresh, on the premises, each morning; soaps are hand-milled. Elizabeth Taylor makes her San Francisco home-away-from-home in the Presidential Suite, as does Mary Tyler Moore. The hotel is conveniently located, with two cable car lines crossing just steps from the main entrance. Business services are available. 905 California St. (phone: 989-3500 or 800-227-4736; fax: 391-0513).

Westin St. Francis A San Francisco landmark since 1904, this hotel has entertained royalty, presidents, and international celebrities with its Old World charm. The 1,200-room establishment still keeps to its traditional theme of red velvet, glimmering crystal, and polished rosewood. At the top of its modern 32-story tower are *Victor's* restaurant, featuring nouvelle cuisine, and the chic *Oz* disco. Both offer lovely panoramas of the city and can be reached via an external elevator that provides spectacular views as it scales the side of the building at 1,000 feet per minute. Afternoon tea is served in the *Compass Rose,* where fluted oak columns, carved ceilings, and antique furnishings harken to a bygone era. Back in the days when society ladies protested that handling coins soiled their white gloves, the hotel provided a coin-washing service for guests. This tradition continues; when you receive change anywhere in the hotel, the coins are so shiny that they seem freshly minted. A fitness center is open daily, room service is available 24 hours a day, and there are numerous amenities geared to businesspeople. 335 Powell St. on Union Sq. (phone: 397-7000 or 800-228-3000; fax: 774-0124).

VERY EXPENSIVE

ANA San Francisco This elegant 36-floor, 667-room establishment (formerly the *Meridien*) is the epitome of commercial luxury on the inside (apparently nothing can be done about the concrete box it comes in). Located in a still-being-developed South of Market area, just a block from the *Moscone Convention Center,* all the rooms have floor-to-ceiling windows with city views. It features a fine restaurant, *Café Fifty-Three,* which serves classic California, Italian, and Japanese dishes; calories can be burned off in the hotel's health club. Business services are available. 50 Third St. (phone: 974-6400 or 800-262-4683; fax: 543-8268).

Campton Place Kempinski Half a block north of Union Square, this small property in the European tradition has 126 sumptuously decorated (but smallish) rooms and suites fitted with armoires, writing desks, cable TV, marble and brass baths, and even padded coat hangers. The service is impeccable. The location—close to shopping, the financial district, and Chinatown—can't be beat. There's a roof garden for sunning and small receptions, and two conference rooms. On the lobby level, wonderfully innovative and well-prepared American dishes are served at breakfast, lunch, and dinner in the *Campton Place* restaurant (see *Eating Out*); cocktails and coffee are available in the adjacent bar. Business services are available. 340 Stockton St. (phone: 781-5555; 800-235-4300 in California; 800-647-4000 elsewhere in the US; fax: 955-8536).

Donatello One block west of Union Square, this elegant hotel offers 94 spacious rooms (including nine suites), a serene atmosphere, and special touches such as plants, terry-cloth robes, valet parking, and a concierge. On the mezzanine level is a restaurant—also called *Donatello*—which serves northern Italian fare. Business services are available. 501 Post St. (phone: 441-7100 or 800-227-3184; fax: 885-8842).

Hyatt Regency Inside this futuristically designed structure is a 17-story atrium lobby with all the activity of a three-ring circus, including a classical guitarist most afternoons and a jazz trio nightly. Glass elevators whisk you to the top, where a revolving restaurant looks out on San Francisco. The 803 rooms are attractive and modern; nonsmoking floors are available. There are numerous services for the business traveler. 5 Embarcadero Center (phone: 788-1234; 800-233-1234 outside California; fax: 398-2567).

Mandarin Oriental This luxurious hostelry occupies the top 11 floors of the 48-story *First Interstate Center* towers in the heart of the financial district, affording each of the 158 rooms unobstructed views of the city and portions of the bay. Glass "sky bridges" connect the two towers. The rooms are graced with Oriental-motif art and marble bathrooms, each one complete with a choice of terry-cloth and lightweight kimono robes, slippers, a digital scale, and a hair dryer. Larger rooms include screened sitting areas and expansive windows. (All offer "On Command Video," a choice of 80 children's and adults' films for a fee.) The marble-walled lobby, the reception area, and the Business Center are all on the ground level. An outstanding restaurant, *Silks,* is on the second floor. Room service is on call 24 hours a day. Business services are available. 222 Sansome St. (phone: 885-0999 or 800-622-0404; fax: 433-0289).

Mark Hopkins Inter-Continental At the height of elegance, crowning Nob Hill, this hotel has a guest list that has included everyone from Haile Selassie to

Frank Sinatra. The 391 suites and rooms feature either classical or contemporary decor, commodious baths and closets, and possibly a grand piano (the Presidential Suite has one). The tower rooms have especially fine views, and the glass-walled *Top of the Mark* lounge offers the best 360° panorama of the city. The *Nob Hill* restaurant (open daily) serves noteworthy California and international fare, with outstanding lamb and duck dishes and wines from 34 states. Business services are available. 1 Nob Hill (phone: 392-3434 or 800-327-0200; fax: 421-3302).

Pan Pacific Glowing with rosy marble, brass, chrome, and glass, this 330-room property combines an American look with Asian-style service. Three valets per floor are on call to unpack, press clothes, polish shoes, draw baths, and prop matchsticks against room doors (a toppled match signals that the guests may be out and their rooms should be tidied up). Exercise machines for in-room use are complimentary, and computers with software can be rented. The menu at the elegant *Pacific Grill* emphasizes the California influence. From 7 AM to 11 PM, Rolls-Royces shuttle guests free of charge to the financial district or to dinner and the theater, and limousines can be rented for airport trips. Business services are available. 500 Post St. (phone: 771-8600 or 800-533-6465; fax: 398-0267).

Prescott A long Oriental carpet on an Italian marble floor leads guests into the reception area of this 167-room establishment, one block from Union Square. Though in the heart of the city, the lobby has the ambience of a gracious Southwestern living room, with its country hearth fireplace and displays of Native American artifacts. The *Postrio* restaurant is hot, with the clientele clamoring for chef Wolfgang Puck's interpretations of classic San Francisco fare (see *Eating Out*). Other amenities include complimentary wine and cheese in the lobby, complimentary limousine service to the financial district on weekday mornings, plus cable TV and stocked refrigerators in the rooms. Business services are available as well. 545 Post St. (phone: 563-0303 or 800-283-7322; fax: 563-6831).

EXPENSIVE

Harbor Court Parallel to the waterfront, this landmark property, built right after the 1906 earthquake, offers Old World charm; 30 of the 131 rooms have bay views (enhanced by the demolition of the Embarcadero Freeway after the 1989 earthquake). The vaulted ceilings and architectural details have been retained throughout the large, club-style lobby and the small, subtly colored guestrooms. Guests have private access to the fully equipped health center and *Harry Denton's* restaurant, located alongside the hotel. Other amenities include limousine service to the financial district each morning, complimentary coffee, tea, and apples served throughout the day, and complimentary wine served each evening from 5 to 7 PM. All rooms have their own refrigerator. There's also a business center; business services are available. 165 Steuart St. (phone: 882-1300 or 800-346-0555).

Miyako This 218-room establishment in Japantown is the place for a plunge into the Orient—and a Japanese bath—especially during the *Cherry Blossom Festival.* The decor is Japanese, but both Japanese- and Western-style suites with saunas are available. The standout fare at the award-winning *Elka* restaurant is seafood cooked the French way but with Asian seasonings. Business services are available. 1625 Post St. (phone: 922-3200 or 800-533-4567; fax: 921-0417).

Petite Auberge Near Union Square but closer to the heart of France, this less pricey Gallic sister of the *White Swan Inn* (see below), complete with an antique carousel horse in the foyer, manages to be both cozy and elegant. A sweeping staircase (and a small elevator for the less athletic) leads to 26 rooms (many with fireplaces) on five floors, furnished in country French style. Full concierge service, a buffet breakfast, afternoon tea, and valet parking are provided; business services also are available. Reserve a month or more in advance. 863 Bush St. (phone: 928-6000; fax: 775-5717).

White Swan Inn Converted from an old hotel, this 26-room English-style inn offers a personal welcome, a lounge and library with fireplaces, plus card rooms and a garden. Rooms are spacious and bright, the amenities luxurious. Full buffet breakfast and afternoon tea, which also includes wine, sherry, and hors d'oeuvres, are complimentary. Valet parking and business services are available. 845 Bush St. (phone: 775-1755; fax: 775-5717).

MODERATE

Andrews This renovated 1905 Victorian building has retained some original brass fixtures and beveled-glass windows, as well as a sense of old-fashioned hospitality, in its 48 rooms. Continental breakfast is included. *Fino,* located off the lobby, serves Italian favorites at dinner. The front desk personnel double as concierges. 624 Post St. (phone: 563-6877 or 800-926-3739; fax: 928-6919).

Bedford Plain on the outside, cheerful with garden colors inside, this 144 room establishment is east of Union Square at the edge of the Tenderloin district. There are still original late-1920s bathroom tiles and fixtures, but more modern amenities include a video library (VCRs in every room), valet parking, complimentary wine in the evening, room service, weekday morning limousine service to the financial district, and business services. The *Canvas Café* serves breakfast. 761 Post St. (phone: 673-6040 or 800-227-5642; fax: 563-6739).

Diva Italianate meets high tech on seven floors with 108 stunning guestrooms, all furnished with chrome, glass, and brightly lacquered furniture and fixtures. The bare floor in the lobby feels cold, and the ultramodern rooms look like a decorator's dream of a "with-it" office, but the theme softens with traditional down comforters and pillows, snacks and cold drinks in the minifridge, and complimentary California breakfast (fresh fruit and multigrain breads, muffins, and cereals along with coffee). Rooms have VCRs, and there is an extensive library of classic and current videos. The *California Pizza Kitchen,* a branch of the "designer pizza" restaurant chain, fits in with the hip Italian theme. Perhaps best of all is the location: right near the theaters and just a couple of blocks from Union Square. Complimentary limousine service is provided to the financial district on weekdays, and other business services are available. 440 Geary St. (phone: 885-0200 or 800-553-1900; fax: 346-6613).

Galleria Park This affordable European-style hostelry between the shopping and financial districts offers 177 rooms and 15 suites (all with refrigerators). (Be aware that the rooms on the lower floors may induce claustrophobia.) There's a third-floor park, a jogging track, an Art Nouveau lobby, and a two-story atrium. Other features, like a concierge, a bar, complimentary morning coffee and wine in the evening, two restaurants (*Bentley's* for fresh seafood and *Brasserie Chambord*), business services, and reasonably priced underground parking, make this place quite impressive for the price. 191 Sutter St. (phone: 781-3060 or 800-792-9639; fax: 433-4409).

The Inn at Union Square Elegant, European-style, and half a block from Union Square, this hotel is for visitors looking for a home away from home. Each of the 30 rooms and suites boasts elegant Georgian furniture—some made in Bath, England—that suggests Thomas Jefferson's *Monticello.* The furniture is set off by warm, colorful fabrics. The lobby and fireplace on each floor provide an ideal setting to enjoy the morning-to-evening parade of complimentary services: continental breakfast, afternoon tea, wine and hors d'oeuvres. No smoking anywhere in the hotel. There are limited business services. 440 Post St. (phone: 397-3510 or 800-288-4346; fax: 989-0529).

Orchard Built in 1907, this restored property near Union Square has an elegant, European look: custom-made Italian rosewood furniture in 96 attractive rooms overlooking a garden. The *Sutter Garden* restaurant serves delicious and reasonably priced breakfast and lunch, with unusually good coffee. Business services are available. 562 Sutter St. (phone: 433-4434 or 800-433-4434; fax: 433-3695).

Richelieu In downtown San Francisco, where old hotels never die, this one has been lovingly restored to the 1906 just-post-earthquake style of its birth. The lobby is rich with antique carpets, settees (the hotel cat may be lounging on its favorite one), mirrors, inverted dome chandeliers, and Tiffany-style stained glass. A piano bar and a small exercise gym are on the premises, and the hotel offers complimentary afternoon tea, though there's no restaurant. Chauffeured limousine service is also complimentary, and business services are available. 1050 Van Ness (phone: 673-4711 or 800-227-3608; fax: 673-9362).

Triton Definitely hip, this 140-room, pastel-decorated establishment in the heart of the gallery district showcases local San Francisco artists. Sophisticated design shows up everywhere—from the hand-painted wall murals to the custom-designed furniture to the staff uniforms. Amenities include CD players and a music library for guests staying in the hotel's moderate-sized ("junior") suites, limousine service to the SoMa district, complimentary wine each evening, bars that serve up plenty of free snacks, and room service. Business services also are available. 342 Grant Ave. (phone: 394-0500 or 800-433-6611; fax: 394-0555).

Victorian Inn on the Park Known as the *Clunie House,* it was built in 1897 in honor of Queen Victoria's *Diamond Jubilee* and now has guests reserving up to a month in advance for one of its 12 bedrooms. Inlaid oak floors, mahogany woodwork, charming period pieces, a handsome oak-paneled dining room (the complimentary continental breakfast features breads baked on the premises), a lavish parlor (complimentary afternoon wine), and off-street parking are only some of the drawing cards of this registered historic landmark. Business services also are available. Across from *Panhandle Park* near *Golden Gate Park* at 301 Lyon St. (phone: 931-1830 or 800-435-1967; fax: 931-1830).

Vintage Court Everything is up-to-date in this 106-room boutique property, established in 1913. (A glass etching of the original building is in the mauve lobby with a cheerful fireplace.) A night's lodging for two costs less than dinner next door at the famed *Masa's* French restaurant (see *Eating Out*); note, however, that the hotel's complimentary continental breakfast is served at *Masa's.* Every afternoon in the lobby, the hotel serves complimentary California wine; weekday limousine service twice a morning to the financial district is also free. Outside rooms (named for Napa Valley wineries) have bay-window seats, padded headboards, and bedspreads in floral or wine-grape motifs. Business services are available. 650 Bush St. (phone: 392-4666 or 800-654-1100; fax: 433-4065).

Washington Square Inn Within walking distance of *Ghirardelli Square* and Chinatown, the turn-of-the-century apartment house–turned-hotel in North Beach has only 15 rooms (10 with private baths), each individually decorated. Three rooms face Washington Square and are more expensive. Complimentary breakfast and afternoon tea are served; there's also a concierge desk. No smoking is permitted in the hotel. 1660 Stockton St. (phone: 981-4220 or 800-388-0220; fax: 397-7242).

INEXPENSIVE

Beresford Here is British charm at a reasonable price: old-fashioned service, a writing parlor off the Victorian lobby, flower boxes in the street windows, and 114 pleasant rooms. Even the lamppost in front has a blue-and-white Wedgwood-esque frieze. Meals served at the *White Horse* tavern here feature fresh vegetables from the hotel's garden. 635 Sutter St. (phone: 673-9900 or 800-533-6533; fax: 474-0449).

Carlton Just five blocks from Union Square, this 165-room property has all the charm of a large home. The hotel's café serves breakfast and dinner daily; complimentary wine is served each evening in the 1920s-style lobby; and room service may be ordered during meal hours. Business services are available. 1075 Sutter St. (phone: 673-0242 or 800-227-4496; fax: 673-4904).

Cornell Everything but the name is French—atmosphere, furnishings, the manager's accent—in this lovingly spruced-up antique, with flower beds behind a picket fence, old reproductions of Cluny tapestries, a cage elevator, and rustic furniture in 55 rooms that have private bathrooms, phones, and cable TV. The *Restaurant Jeanne d'Arc,* filled with memorabilia honoring its namesake, serves dinner six days a week and complimentary breakfast. Some business services are available. Ask about the special weekly rate. Smoking is prohibited. 715 Bush St. (phone: 421-3154 or 800-232-9698; fax: 399-1442).

Dakota Two blocks from Union Square, this 1920 historic landmark hotel has 41 rooms. Geared for budget travelers, it has spacious claw-foot bathtubs but, otherwise, no frills. 606 Post St. (phone: 931-7475).

Golden Gate This is another renovated relic, owned and run by a very friendly, multilingual couple. Period photographs and the cage elevator hark back to the hotel's 1913 beginnings, but the small, comfortable rooms are fresh and bright, with flowered wallpaper and white wicker furniture or mahogany antiques. Of the 23 rooms, 14 have private baths, and nine share three baths in the halls. Continental breakfast and afternoon tea are served in a cheery lounge with a fireplace. There's a concierge, too. 775 Bush St. (phone: 392-3702 or 800-835-1118; fax: 392-6202).

EATING OUT

San Francisco has about 4,300 eating places, serving a wide variety of food, from haute cuisine to ethnic fare, and taking fine advantage of the wonderful seafood and fresh produce so readily available from the ocean and the surrounding valleys. Along with such longtime favorites as *Ernie's* and *Jack's,* San Franciscans welcome new restaurants that show up on the horizon at an astonishing rate. One notable trend is toward first-rate food in hotels, starting with *Campton Place* and extending to even newer establishments like *Postrio* at the *Prescott* hotel. At the other end of the spectrum are the neighborhood places that specialize in Chinese, Japanese, Vietnamese, Thai, or Mexican food at very affordable prices. Our restaurant selections range in price from $75 or more (sometimes much more) for dinner for two in the expensive category; to $45 to $75, moderate; to less than $45, inexpensive—excluding drinks, wine, and tip. Unless otherwise noted, all telephone numbers are in the 415 area code, and all restaurants are open for both lunch and dinner.

For an unforgettable dining experience, we begin with our culinary favorites, followed by our cost and quality choices, listed by price category.

INCREDIBLE EDIBLES

Chez Panisse The oft-called "guru of California cookery," Alice Waters, opened this landmark restaurant in the early 1970s. Set in a house in Berkeley, it has a sparse, redwood-beamed dining room where the limited menu offerings reflect the southern French and northern Italian influences on West Coast dishes. The place may be no longer in its heyday, but devotees still make a pilgrimage here. Since only one meal is served in the downstairs dining room each evening, you may want to call ahead to find out if it will be spring lamb, grilled salmon, ravioli stuffed with potatoes, or something even more innovative. Upstairs the more casual and less expensive *Chez Panisse Café* specializes in pizza, *calzones,* salads, and soups. Closed Sundays. Reservations necessary at least a month in advance. Major credit cards accepted. 1517 Shattuck Ave., Berkeley (phone: 510-548-5525).

Ernie's Walking into this multi-star restaurant is like stepping into a warm, inviting Victorian home. Ernie Carlesso opened his now-famous establishment in 1934; the sons of his original partner continue the tradition. Champagne silk wall coverings and elaborately carved woodwork set the tone for tuxedoed waiters to serve contemporary French dishes; a one-bite appetizer is served as soon as diners are seated. Menu offerings include leek salad with osetra caviar and lemon cream, Dungeness crab cakes with tomato gelée, roast duck or *confit* of duck, salmon tartare, venison *au poivre,* and roulades of veal or tuna. For the undecided there is the *menu dégustation* combining three appetizers, two entrées, and dessert. Petits fours and cookies are served at the end of every meal. The wine list is extensive: a 17,000-bottle inventory. Open for dinner only; closed Sundays. Reservations advised. Major credit cards accepted. 847 Montgomery St. (phone: 397-5969).

Fleur de Lys One of the oldest French restaurants in the city, it boasts an incredibly romantic setting, with murals and 700 yards of red and green floral fabric decorating the dining area. Though the fare is French (and pricey), there are definite California influences, with the presentation equaling the preparation. The menu features such dishes as coconut soup with lobster, corn pancakes with salmon, and roast loin of lamb with parsnip flan. Open for dinner only; closed Sundays. Valet parking is available.

Reservations advised. Major credit cards accepted. 777 Sutter St. (phone: 673-7779).

Fog City Diner Mention the word "diner," and what comes to mind? BLTs? Gum-chomping waitresses? Pot-bellied short-order cooks? Not so here. This 1930s Pullman-style eatery is sleek, unique, and perennially packed. Created by chef Cindy Pawlcyn (who also opened *Mustard's* in Napa and several Carmel Valley restaurants), the food and the ambience—dazzling chrome and neon—are dramatically different from that found in a traditional American diner. Chicly dressed patrons like to order appetizer-size plates of red curry mussel stew and crab cakes and play smorgasbord. A meal here generally will run less than at the other restaurants listed in this section. Open daily. Reservations advised. Major credit cards accepted. 1300 Battery St. (phone: 982-2000).

Lark Creek Inn In the kitchen of a historic Victorian house across the bay in Marin County, chef Bradley Ogden combines fresh meat and produce from local farms to create fine regional American fare. A wood-burning oven enhances the flavors of baked and roasted entrées; breads and desserts are made on the premises; and the outstanding wine list offers more than 200 selections. Expansive windows afford panoramic views of redwood trees and gardens; in warm weather, the patio along Lark Creek is open for dining. Closed Saturdays for lunch; Sunday brunch instead of lunch. Reservations advised. Major credit cards accepted. 234 Magnolia Ave., Larkspur (phone: 924-7766).

Masa's Although Masa Kobayshi died in 1985, his namesake restaurant, headed by protégé Julian Serrano, still ranks as one of the city's finest. Masa was a master of creative combinations, extravagant sauces, and perfect presentation, and Serrano carries on that tradition. The menu changes daily. Highlights might include grilled scallops with saffron sauce, sautéed medallions of fallow deer with caramelized apples and zinfandel sauce, or roast squab with risotto. For dessert order the sublime white and dark chocolate mousse with raspberry sauce or the unique baked apple in phyllo pastry with cinnamon-rosemary ice cream. Open Tuesdays through Saturdays, 6 to 9:30 PM. Reservations necessary; call three weeks ahead. Major credit cards accepted. 648 Bush St. (phone: 989-7154).

Postrio Elegant and airy (and expensive), this dining place in the *Prescott* hotel is the creation of a talented trio: chef-restaurateur Wolfgang Puck, of *Spago* fame, and Anne and David Gingrass, former chefs at *Spago*. Nightly specials feature California's freshest ingredients, prepared with Asian and Mediterranean influences. Favorite dishes include grilled baby lamb chops on wilted salad with cilantro honey vinaigrette, and roast salmon with almond–black pepper crust and warm spinach salad. Pizza, salads, and sandwiches are served upstairs at the bar. A ribbon theme—which ties together three levels and a grand staircase—runs throughout the restaurant. Lighting fixtures, incorporating hand-blown glass ribbons, were created by a former jewelry designer. Service is impeccable. Open daily for all three meals. It's gotten a bit easier to get in, but book as far ahead as possible (reservations unnecessary for the bar or for breakfast). Major credit cards accepted. 545 Post St. (phone: 776-7825).

Square One Joyce Goldstein, an alumna of *Chez Panisse* (see above), brings together flavors from Portugal, Italy, North Africa, as well as other areas of the Mediterranean in this Bay City dining place. The à la carte menu changes regularly, depending on what's fresh. An open cooking area makes it easy for guests to watch chefs at work. Bread, desserts, and ice cream are made on the premises, and the wine list is extensive. Closed for lunch on weekends. Reservations advised. Major credit cards accepted. 190 Pacific Ave. (phone: 788-1110).

Stars Colorful, energetic, and sometimes a bit noisy, this is a gathering place for the city's rich and famous. Jeremiah Tower, another graduate of *Chez Panisse,* prepares American classics with contemporary flair—veal shanks, venison, fish (even hamburgers, hot dogs, and pizza). Though the setting is elegant, the mood is casual, and diners come dressed in everything from black tie to blue jeans. Sit at the long, long bar (48 feet), listen to the piano player, and watch the chefs in the open kitchen prepare your meal. The menu changes daily; small eaters are advised to skip the appetizer and save room for dessert. It's open late and within walking distance of the *Opera House* and *Symphony Hall.* Open daily. Reservations advised. Major credit cards accepted. 150 Redwood Alley, between Polk St. and Van Ness Ave. (phone: 861-7827).

EXPENSIVE

Aqua In the financial district, this dramatic dining place—peach-colored walls, huge floral arrangements—features innovative seafood dishes such as ravioli stuffed with a creamy lobster salad, and medallions of *ahi* tuna. Valet parking. Closed Saturdays for lunch and Sundays. Reservations necessary. Major credit cards accepted. 252 California St. (phone: 956-9662).

Campton Place Although it's in the *Campton Place Kempinski* hotel, this is a legitimate magnet for diners in its own right. The relatively small room is decorated in soft shades of rose and gray, while the menu is an outstanding example of American dishes done to perfection—without excessive fuss or fanfare. Breakfast (arguably the best in the city), lunch, and dinner are served daily, and each is marvelous. Reservations at least a week in advance are necessary. Major credit cards accepted. 340 Stockton St. (phone: 781-5555).

Geordy's From the time it opened its doors late in 1992, this contemporary dining room has delivered consistently well-prepared seasonal dishes. The menu changes, but monkfish with ricotta gnocchi and brioche-stuffed roast chicken surrounded by mushrooms rate raves. This eatery is as well suited to shoppers looking for a light lunch as to business folk on expense accounts. Closed Sundays. Reservations necessary. Major credit cards accepted. 1 Tillman Pl., off Grant Ave. between Sutter and Post Sts. (phone: 362-3175).

Harris' There are still places to go in San Francisco that feature a basic meat-and-potatoes meal with excellent service. Here the dark oak paneling and leather banquettes help create the quiet aura of an elegant men's club. The emphasis is beef: thick steaks and prime ribs aged for 21 days in a refrigerator to intensify their flavor. But leave room for dessert—the chocolate decadence torte is sinful. Open for dinner daily, for lunch on Wednesdays only. Reservations advised. Major credit cards accepted. 2100 Van Ness Ave. (phone 673-1888).

Zuni Café The fare at this casual brick and glass, California-Mediterranean–style dining spot (with sidewalk tables, too) changes daily; it's based on the seasonal ingredients chef Judy Rodgers finds at the market each morning. The eclectic menu features the cuisine of southern France with an emphasis on braised meat and poultry and grilled seafood; pasta is also a favorite, and there is an oyster bar. Closed Mondays; open for all three meals the rest of the week. Reservations advised. Major credit cards accepted. 1658 Market St. (phone: 552-2522).

MODERATE

Angkor Wat Expand your Oriental horizons at this Cambodian dining place where specialties include prawn soup, codfish, and curried chicken. The *Cambodian Classical Ballet* performs here on Friday and Saturday nights. Closed Mondays. Reservations unnecessary. Major credit cards accepted. 4127 Geary Blvd. (phone: 221-7887).

China Moon In a cleverly disguised coffee shop setting, owner/chef Barbara Tropp has succeeded in presenting her singular brand of Chinese food. In what other "Chinese" restaurant would you expect to find such appetizers as chili-spiked spring rolls, spicy lamb, fresh water chestnuts, and Peking antipasto plates side by side with a California wine list and Western-style desserts? Portions are small; no smoking is permitted. Closed Sundays for lunch. Reservations advised. MasterCard and Visa accepted. 639 Post St. (phone: 775-4789).

Flying Saucer Out of this world in more ways than one, this tiny place (19 tables) decorated with UFO-style memorabilia dishes out huge salads and such heavenly entrées as duck *confit* in coconut-lemongrass lentil sauce and sautéed black sea bass. Open Tuesdays through Saturdays for dinner only. Because of its popularity—and its limited number of tables—reserve ahead and be willing to take the last of three nightly seatings. No credit cards accepted. 1000 Guerrero St. (phone: 641-9955).

Gordon Biersch Brewery The financial district meets South of Market at this classy bar and restaurant on *The Embarcadero.* Featured are pitchers of house ales and a bar menu that's long on pizza; restaurant fare ranges from braised lamb shanks to wild mushroom risotto. Open daily. Reservations advised for dinner. Major credit cards accepted. 2 Harrison St. (phone: 243-8246).

Greens Devotees consider this vegetarian eatery the best in the country. Things are always what they seem here; nothing masquerades as meat. Sandwiches, pizza, pasta, chili, salad, and five-course prix fixe dinners on weekends are enhanced by fine views across the marina to the *Golden Gate Bridge.* Closed Mondays; open for brunch only on Sundays. Reservations advised. Major credit cards accepted. *Fort Mason,* Bldg. A (phone: 771-6222).

Happy Immortal This Chinese eatery in the city's Richmond district serves some of the best Hunan crab around. If you're going with a group, try the whole chicken stuffed with sweet rice; delicious and quite reasonable (about $25 for six people), this dish must be ordered in advance. Closed Wednesdays. Reservations necessary on weekends. MasterCard and Visa accepted. 4401 Cabrillo St. (phone: 386-7538).

Hayes Street Grill In a city famous for its seafood restaurants, this is one of the best—a quintessential San Francisco dining experience. Everything is fresh; nothing is overcooked. There always is a long list of daily specials, along with great sourdough bread and an unusually good *crème brûlée* for dessert. Closed for lunch on weekends. Reservations advised; consider dining here after performances start at nearby venues. Major credit cards accepted. 320 Hayes St. (phone: 863-5545).

Jack's This excellent continental restaurant has been a landmark for nearly as long as San Francisco has been on the map, but because it's in the financial district, it's unknown to many visitors. All the grilled entrées are recommended, and for dessert the banana fritters with brandy sauce are unbeatable. The decor is unpretentious, as are the prices (particularly the dinner special), and the service is good. Open weekdays for lunch only, Saturdays for dinner only; closed Sundays. Reservations necessary. American Express accepted. 615 Sacramento St. (phone: 421-7355).

Kyung Bok Palace For fanciers of Korea's *kimchee* (spicy pickled cabbage) and grilled meat and seafood, this place is San Francisco's finest. Chicken, pork, shrimp, baby octopus, and thinly sliced beef are presented at a buffet, and you can cook selections at your table's own grill. There is no menu, and the price is fixed for all you can eat. Open daily. Reservations necessary. MasterCard and Visa accepted. 6314 Geary Blvd. (phone: 221-0685).

McCormick & Kuleto's A wall of windows provides breathtaking views of San Francisco Bay from this *Ghirardelli Square* eatery. The emphasis is on seafood, with the list of fresh fish and oysters on the half shell changing daily. There's an extensive wine list, and valet parking is available. Open daily. Reservations advised. Major credit cards accepted. 900 North Point (phone: 929-1730).

Pane e Vino The extension of a Santa Barbara establishment, this authentic-looking trattoria features such northern Italian fare as *vitello tonnato* (sliced veal with a sauce of tuna, mayonnaise, and capers), risotto, and grilled fish. It's close to the Triangle area of singles bars, so parking spots are at a premium. Closed Sundays for lunch. Reservations necessary. MasterCard and Visa accepted. 3011 Steiner St. (phone: 346-2111).

Tadich Grill San Francisco's oldest restaurant (ca. 1849) is still going strong with what folks maintain is the freshest seafood in town. Best bets: baked avocado with shrimp *diablo,* rex sole, salmon, and sea bass. Don't pass up the homemade cheesecake for dessert. Open only until 9 PM; closed Sundays and major holidays. No reservations. MasterCard and Visa accepted. 240 California St. (phone: 391-1849).

Wu Kong Far beyond the fringes of Chinatown, Shanghai-style food is served in a well-appointed dining room with a nice atmosphere. Seafood and vegetable dishes are fresh and well prepared. Open daily. Reservations advised. Major credit cards accepted. 101 Spear St. at *Rincon Center* (phone: 957-9300).

Yoshida-Ya This stunning Japanese spot is known for its excellent *yakitori*—a selection of meat, fish, and vegetables, all marinated, skewered, and grilled over charcoal. Upstairs is less crowded, as are weekends. Open daily. Reservations necessary. Major credit cards accepted. 2909 Webster St. at Union St. (phone: 346-3431).

INEXPENSIVE

Angkor Borei Adventurous diners might enjoy the unusually prepared seafood at this Cambodian eatery. Open daily. Reservations advised on weekends. Major credit cards accepted. 3471 Mission St. (phone: 550-8417).

Burma's House Among the myriad Chinese dishes listed on the extensive menu, there are some unusual—and delicious—Burmese specialties, such as *pat dok* (a salad of fermented tea leaves, toasted lentils, ground shrimp, green chilies, garlic, and sesame seeds) and *moo hing nga* (a traditional Burmese fish chowder with rice noodles, chilies, tamarind, hard-boiled egg, and kernels of corn). Open daily. Reservations necessary on weekends. MasterCard and Visa accepted. 720 Post St. (phone: 775-1156).

Casa Aguila At this haven of south-of-the-border warmth in the fog-shrouded Sunset district, try seafood prepared tableside on the *parrilla* (small grill); portions are large enough to fill several doggie bags. Open daily. No reservations; you wait outside on the street. Major credit cards accepted. 1240 Noriega St. between 19th and 20th Aves. (phone: 661-5593).

Far East Café Don't let the neon-lit exterior fool you—inside are ornate Chinese lanterns and private, curtained booths. The extensive Cantonese and Mandarin menu features all the old classics and, if you call in advance, an excellent family banquet. Open daily. Reservations advised. Major credit cards accepted. 631 Grant Ave. (phone: 982-3245).

Fly Trap In the trendy SoMa district, this is a re-creation of a turn-of-the-century restaurant that earned its nickname from the squares of flypaper flapping over each table. The flypaper is gone, but the name has stuck; the menu has Californian flair and the nostalgic flavor of old San Francisco, with hearty original dishes. Valet parking. Closed Saturdays for lunch and Sundays. Reservations advised. Major credit cards accepted. 606 Folsom St. (phone: 243-0580).

Isobune There's only counter service at these two sushi and sashimi spots—but what counter service! Japanese-style wooden boats glide by bearing all sorts of wonders, and patrons take what they want. The tab is figured by counting plates. Open daily. No reservations; expect a wait. MasterCard and Visa accepted. 1737 Post St. (phone: 563-1030) and 1451 Burlingame Ave., Burlingame (phone: 344-8433).

Jackson Fillmore Garlicky, steamy, cozy, and informal, this Pacific Heights trattoria is a favorite among locals for early Sunday evening meals. Specialties include osso buco (braised veal shanks); chicken sautéed with tomatoes, olives, onions, and anchovies; and a wide variety of pasta. Open daily for dinner only. Reservations advised for parties of three or more; let them know if you will take a place at the counter. Major credit cards accepted. 2506 Fillmore St. (phone: 346-5288).

Pacific Vietnamese owner Ninh Nguyen prides himself on his *pho*, a beef noodle soup with shallots, ginger, cinnamon, and *nuoc mam*, the Vietnamese version of soy sauce. Also on this creative menu are a good selection of fish and beef dishes—all at extremely reasonable prices. Open daily for breakfast and lunch only. No reservations or credit cards accepted. 607 Larkin St. (phone: 441-6722).

San Francisco Bar-B-Q The aroma of Thai spices wafts over Potrero Hill when the cooks fire up the grill to barbecue spareribs, chicken, salmon, trout, lamb, or even oysters. The meat can be ordered à la carte or as part of a dinner that includes sticky rice, grated carrot salad, and sourdough bread. A bowl of noodles comes cooked in sesame and soy, with crisp grilled pieces of duck. Just about everything on the menu can be ordered to go. Closed

Sundays for lunch and Mondays. No reservations or credit cards accepted. 1328 18th St. (phone: 431-8956).

Sears Fine Food A line forms outside on summer mornings at this San Francisco institution serving old-fashioned breakfasts. The pancakes are Swedish; the French toast is made with sourdough bread. The standard lunch menu includes such nonstandard items as lemon soufflé. Open for breakfast and lunch, Wednesdays through Sundays. No reservations or credit cards accepted (avoid a wait by sitting at the counter). 439 Powell St. (phone: 986-1160).

Straits Café Direct from Singapore come such Oriental delicacies as *achar* (pickled vegetables), *kari lembu* (beef curry), *patong kari ayam* (coconut-curry chicken), as well as *satays* and chili crab. Open daily. Reservations advised on weekends. Major credit cards accepted. 3300 Geary Blvd. (phone: 668-1783).

Diversions

Diversions

Exceptional Pleasures and Treasures

Quintessential San Francisco

According to author William Saroyan, in San Francisco "every block is a short story, every hill a novel." As you wander around and through its full-of-character (and character-filled) streets, you can watch its stories unfold: a mime acting out a scene at the cable car turntable at *Aquatic Park,* a motorist trying to maneuver through the throngs along Chinatown's Grant Avenue, a couple from the East catching their first look at a redwood tree. A city where not only Tony Bennett "left his heart," San Francisco (please don't call it "Frisco") is more than just a magnificent hilly city surrounded by an incredibly blue bay—it's an experience that stays with you long after the song has ended.

POINTS OF VIEW San Francisco is an "ooh" and "ahh" kind of place—there's a special vista around just about every corner and each time you look over your shoulder. "Ooh." Driving down Mason Street from the top of Nob Hill is an act of faith—is the pavement really there? "Ahh." As the sun sets, the warm glow of the dome of the *Palace of Fine Arts* against the deep blue sky leaves a lasting impression. The snippets are dazzling; the whole picture—the bay, the bridges, the skyline—will take your breath away.

Ferries traversing San Francisco Bay are the best way to see the city from the water. Ferry service began in 1830, to serve the Franciscan fathers who helped found the city. As the post–Gold Rush city grew, day-trippers and vacationers crossed the bay by ferry to escape the summer fog and find the warming sunshine in Marin County and the East Bay. By the time the San Francisco–Oakland Bay Bridge opened in 1936 and the *Golden Gate Bridge* in 1937, 50 giant ferries carried 50 million passengers across the bay each year.

Today ferries are enjoying a renaissance; commuters, tired of rush-hour traffic, are opting for a boat ride to work. But there's no need to be heading anywhere special. Glassed-in observation areas and open promenade decks make it easy to enjoy the view; food and drink are sold on board.

Cross the San Francisco–Oakland Bay Bridge for another perspective on "The City by the Bay." Treasure Island (manmade for the *1939–1940 Golden Gate International Exposition*) is a US Navy post; from the parking area just outside the sentry gate, the skyline stretches from bridge to bridge. Between them stand the Transamerica Pyramid, *Coit Tower,* the Bank of America World Headquarters building, and other recognizable landmarks.

Stunning views can also be enjoyed from inside a jet-engine helicopter that whirs its way over the *Golden Gate Bridge,* the San Francisco–Oakland Bay Bridge, *Fisherman's Wharf,* and Treasure Island. The 30-minute, fully narrated tour departs from *Oakland International Airport,* with complimentary pick-up service from city hotels and *Fisherman's Wharf (San Francisco Helicopter Tours;* phone: 800-400-2404). Once you've come down to earth, this is a heavenly city for walkers.

RIDING A CABLE CAR More scenic than any roller coaster ride, a short hop on one of these colorful, bell-clanging classic cars is probably the best way to get a sense of downtown. A tourist's treat and a commuter's lifeline, they carry camera-toting tourists from Topeka and briefcase-laden bankers from Montgomery Street to their destinations—all for a mere $2.

The idea of burying cables beneath the streets of the city that would pull small cars up and down San Francisco's steep hills dates back to 1873, with credit going to Andrew Hallidie. In its heyday, before the 1906 earthquake, the cable car system included 600 cars traveling over 110 miles of cable. Today 39 cars cover only 4.4 miles, carrying some 13 million travelers every year. Of the three currently operating lines—California, Powell-Mason, and Powell-Hyde—the last, which connects *Aquatic Park* with the corner of Powell and Market Streets, is generally considered to be the most exciting ride. The California line has the largest cars and is least crowded.

DRIVING DOWN LOMBARD STREET A short note on an even shorter street: Nicknamed "the crookedest street in the world," this narrow, practically vertical, serpentine stretch between Hyde and Leavenworth Streets is lined with charming homes decorated with flower-filled window boxes. A mere 500 feet in length, Lombard Street has eight hairpin turns—hard on car brakes, it's even harder on the calf muscles. No matter how you choose to see it, this is a must. To avoid summer afternoon congestion, approach southbound on Hyde Street.

CLIMBING FILBERT STEPS A brass plaque on a bench along these steps reads, "I have a feeling we're not in Kansas anymore." You can say that again! San Francisco's Filbert Steps—and its tributary lanes, which climb a slope of Telegraph Hill—is one of the city's hidden treasures. Tiny wooden houses—Gold Rush–era saloons, grocery stores, and shanties—are visible through lush gardens of roses, calla lilies, azaleas, and purple plumeria, depending on the season. Dating back to the period from 1875 to 1890, these cottages are among the very few structures in this part of the city that survived the 1906 earthquake and fires. (Legend has it that their inhabitants covered the roofs with wine-soaked rags to fend off the flames.) It's hard to believe that these gardens, where flowers bloom and birds twitter, sit on the site of a former dump. Grace Marchant, to whom they are dedicated, devoted 30 years of her life to reclaiming, replanting, and tending this secret jewel.

To climb the Filbert Steps, follow Sansome Street north across Broadway, and park near Levi Plaza. Follow the steps up, making sure to look down Napier Lane and Darrell Place. When you reach the top, you'll find some wonderful wide-angle views of the bay from *Coit Tower*. Trust us—the view is well worth the climb. (To explore the steps from the top down, see *Walk 3: North Beach* in DIRECTIONS.)

SUNDAY IN GOLDEN GATE PARK Built on bare sand dunes over a hundred years ago, this 3-mile-long, 1,017-acre park is at its best on a sunny Sunday—when some of its roads are closed to traffic and taken over by joggers, bicyclists, skaters, and strollers. Sunday or any day there's something for everyone: band concerts, museums, an aquarium, and an arboretum. San Franciscans have been coming here since the 1870s, traveling by train, trolley, and horse-drawn carriage to partake of this serene setting. Dotted with lakes and gardens (including a Japanese tea garden), the park also boasts athletic fields of all sorts, windmills, fly-casting pools, a riding stable, and even a buffalo paddock. For leisurely walks or just plain people watching, this verdant span rates right up there with Paris's *Tuileries.*

DIM SUM It's no secret that some of the best dim sum outside of Hong Kong can be found in San Francisco. Though the decor of most dim sum restaurants is bare-boned (Formica tables crammed together), the food—a Chinese smorgasbord of appetizers served on tiny dishes—is dizzying but delicious. More a "happening" than an ordinary meal, this is a repast to be enjoyed at leisure. Allow ample time to sample the offerings—pork and shrimp dumplings, spring rolls, steamed pork buns, and fried taro cakes. Waiters push delicacy-laden carts, allowing you to point and pick until you've had your fill. The tab for this unique dining experience is surprisingly low—between $10 and $15 per person (to calculate the cost, servers count the number of saucers on the table). Here are two of the best dim sum sites, both upscale and outside Chinatown: *Mandarin* at *Ghirardelli Square* (900 North Point; phone: 415-673-8812) and *Harbor Village* in *Embarcadero Center Four* (at Front St.; phone: 415-781-8833).

NORTH BEACH CAFÉS From early morning until late at night, the tiny tables of the North Beach cafés are full. The air is abuzz—it always feels like something important or interesting is about to happen. Each occupant is a vignette: There are the writers sipping cappuccino *grandes* as they scribble in their notebooks; the intellectuals arguing world philosophy; the newspaper readers; the tired; the lonely; the people watchers. *Caffè Trieste* (601 Vallejo St.; phone: 415-392-6739) tops the list as far as character goes. This is one of the last—and for some, the greatest—bastions of the Beat Era. Jack Kerouac and Allen Ginsberg drank espresso here some four decades ago. Francis Ford Coppola reportedly edited the film script for *The Godfather* here. Though the *Trieste* is crowded every day of the week, Saturday afternoons are best, when the regular patrons show off their operatic skills. The narrow maze of North Beach streets is full of cafés. One block away is *Caffè Puccini* (411 Columbus Ave.; phone: 415-989-7033). Open the door and the sounds of Puccini's music—coming from the jukebox—fill the air. Across the street restored frescoes and murals adorn the walls of *Caffè Roma* (414 Columbus Ave.; phone: 415-391-8584). Indulge the urge to order a *caffè latte* and become part of the North Beach scene.

A Few of Our Favorite Things

This city is known for its great hotels and restaurants, enchanting urban vistas both in town and along the coast, and great outdoor opportunities—the famous fog notwithstanding.

Each place listed below is described in greater detail in THE CITY chapter.

GRAND HOTELS AND SPECIAL HAVENS

The following are our accommodation favorites. Complete information about our choices can be found on pages 60 to 63 of THE CITY chapter.

Archbishop's Mansion Inn
Fairmont
Four Seasons Clift
Huntington
Inn at the Opera
Ritz-Carlton
Sheraton Palace
Sherman House
Stouffer–Stanford Court
Westin St. Francis

INCREDIBLE EDIBLES

This sophisticated yet warmhearted city sustains a number of fine chefs schooled in myriad cooking styles, including classics such as French cuisine plus a superb blend of American and Asian influences. The following are our picks of the top eateries here. Complete information about our choices can be found on pages 70 to 72 of THE CITY chapter.

Chez Panisse, Berkeley
Ernie's
Fleur de Lys
Fog City Diner
Lark Creek Inn, Larkspur (Marin County)
Masa's
Postrio
Square One
Stars

San Francisco's Sounds of Music

San Francisco offers an eclectic mix of music—from a world class symphony and opera to the best in blues, jazz, and rock. The clubs are alive every night of the week, and outdoor concerts are standard summer fare. The *Bay Guardian* and *SF Weekly,* two free publications that can be found on many street corners, offer current listings for the weekly music scene. Indoors or out, no matter what the season, in San Francisco there's music for everyone.

SAN FRANCISCO OPERA Considered second in the United States only to New York City's *Metropolitan Opera,* this is as grand as grand opera gets. Sets are elaborate, costumes are ornate, and performances are presented in the original language with English translations projected above the stage so the audience can follow the action. Not a museum for operatic classics, programming includes 17th-century operas and contemporary works, as well as its standard repertory. Many now-famous artists—including Leontyne Price—launched their careers with the *San Francisco Opera.* Luciano Pavarotti is also a familiar presence on this stage. The opening of the opera season (the first Friday after *Labor Day*), with its benefit ball and gala performance, is as much a show as any of the staged productions. Tickets for the 3,100-seat *War Memorial Opera House,* part of the *Civic Center,* sell out quickly; standing room, however, is almost always available. Information: *San Francisco Opera, War Memorial Opera House,* Van Ness Ave. and Grove St. (phone: 415-864-3330).

SAN FRANCISCO SYMPHONY Programming at *Davies Symphony Hall* reflects the diversity of musical tastes and trends in San Francisco. The subscription series (which runs from September through May) features top-name guest artists. The Great Performers series brings visiting orchestras and recitalists to the concert hall; less conventional programs have included Bobby McFerrin conducting the symphony, and English violinist Nigel Kennedy playing classical and rock violin music. Pops concerts and performances by the *Joffrey Ballet* make up part of the summer schedule. The symphony's 9,235-pipe Ruffatti organ is the largest concert hall organ in North America. Tours of *Louise M. Davies Symphony Hall,* part of the *Civic Center,* are given on Wednesdays and Saturdays (phone: 415-552-8338). Information: *San Francisco Symphony,* Van Ness Ave. and Grove St. (phone: 415-431-5400).

BEACH BLANKET BABYLON San Francisco has the sublime (see above), and then it has the ridiculous, as in this farcical revue. The current musical production features Snow White encountering a star-studded lineup of hilarious characters during a fast-paced, around-the-world quest for a prince. Wild costumes and giant towering hats that light up add to the zaniness. Seating is cabaret style; beer, wine, and desserts are served. Reservations necessary. Information: *Beach Blanket Babylon, Club Fugazi,* 678 Green St. (phone: 415-421-4222).

STERN GROVE MIDSUMMER MUSIC FESTIVAL What could be more enticing, more peaceful, than a midsummer concert in a meadow surrounded by a grove of redwood, eucalyptus, and pine trees? That's the setting for the free music series presented here at 2 PM every Sunday throughout the summer. There's a classical emphasis—symphony, opera, ballet; and ethnic music and dance programs, an occasional Gilbert and Sullivan operetta, and groups such as the *Preservation Hall Jazz Band* round out the schedule. Regulars come early to find the best blanket spot (you should, too); picnic baskets are in order here. Information: *Sigmund Stern Grove,* 19th Ave. and Sloat Blvd. (phone: 415-252-6252).

AUDIUM People don't walk out of here humming a tune. In this, the only theater of its kind, you sit in total darkness and watch what its creators call "sound sculptures and sound paintings." Using a combination of natural and synthetic sounds played through 136 speakers embedded in the walls, under the seats, and suspended from the ceiling, the 75-minute show takes its audience on a unique aural adventure. Shows are Fridays and Saturdays at 8:30 PM. Information: *Audium,* 1616 Bush St. (phone: 415-771-1616).

GREAT AMERICAN MUSIC HALL Built in 1907, right after the great earthquake, this popular nightspot was a bordello before it was a music club. Some of that historical grandeur has been retained in the red and mirrored walls and the gold trim of its Baroque-style interior. As for the music, it's just like the name says; expect to find a wide variety of jazz, blues, rock, and folk. Artists such as Etta James, John Lee Hooker, Carmen McRae, and Queen Ida have all graced the stage here; for a while this was the only place Van Morrison would play in the United States. The hall is small; the atmosphere, intimate; seating is on a first-come, first-served basis. Depending on the program, space may be set aside for a dance floor. Hamburgers, sandwiches, and a full bar are available. Information: *Great American Music Hall,* 859 O'Farrell St. (phone: 415-885-0750).

KIMBALL'S EAST Big-name talent—such as Lou Rawls, Eartha Kitt, Maynard Ferguson, and the *Stylistics*—is usually booked into this Emeryville club (located in the East Bay between Oakland and Berkeley). Designed to be a jazz club, it has table seating on multiple levels, tiered down to a stage. This place is known among jazz aficionados as a first-rate nightspot. Information: *Kimball's East,* 5800 Shellmound Ave. at the *EmeryBay Public Market,* Emeryville (the first exit, Powell St., off I-80 east after crossing the Bay Bridge; phone: 510-658-2555).

YOSHI'S NIGHT SPOT One of the premier jazz clubs in the Bay Area, it presents straight-ahead jazz and Latin dance music. Don't expect to find the artist on the cutting edge playing experimental music here. Instead, *Yoshi's* attracts established artists with a traditional bent. The decor is Japanese, and the menu, which includes sushi, offers a combination of Japanese and California cooking. Tickets can be purchased at the club or through *BASS* ticket outlets (phone: 510-762-BASS). Dance nights carry a cover charge; there's free parking. Information: *Yoshi's Night Spot,* 6030 Claremont Ave., Oakland (phone: 510-652-9200).

SLIM'S In 1988, musician Boz Scaggs and about half a dozen others in the music business set out to create a solid rhythm-and-blues club in a converted warehouse featuring a custom-designed sound system. Since opening, the club has featured western, Cajun, and African music, as well as rock. Such talent as Rickie Lee Jones, Albert Collins, and Bonnie Raitt play here. Food is served, but it's limited to snacks such as chicken wings, nachos, and pizza. Music is played most nights; all ages are welcome. Seating varies depending on the show, but a dance floor is opened up when appropriate. Tickets can be purchased at the door or through *BASS* ticket outlets (phone: 510-762-BASS). Information: *Slim's,* 333 11th St. (phone: 415-621-3330).

FREIGHT AND SALVAGE COFFEE HOUSE For the past 24 years, this Berkeley mainstay operated by the nonprofit *Berkeley Society for the Preservation of Traditional Music* has offered the finest in folk music. A few years ago bigger and better quarters were opened, and now about 220 people can be accommodated in cabaret-style seating. Recent names to grace the stage include Tom Paxton, Utah Phillips, John Lewis Walker, and Dan Hicks. Tuesday is open mike night; anyone can come onstage and play. There's no drinking or smoking, but a snack bar is available. Advance tickets are usually a good idea and can be purchased at *BASS* ticket outlets (phone: 510-762-BASS) or at the box office. Information: *Freight and Salvage,* 1111 Addison St., Berkeley (phone: 510-548-1761).

Glorious Gardens

The landscaped face of *Golden Gate Park* is largely the result of the efforts of one man: John McLaren. As "boss gardener" for 56 years (from 1887 to 1943), his love of plants, his commitment to open space, and his tenacious spirit helped shape what are probably the most beloved and best-used thousand acres in all of San Francisco. One need not have a green thumb to enjoy the trees, shrubs, and flowers that grow abundantly on what were once barren sand dunes. Explore the entire park—gardens, lakes, verdant meadows, and woodlands (see *Walk 7: Golden Gate Park* in DIRECTIONS)—or sample just these three very different garden settings.

CONSERVATORY OF FLOWERS This "Crystal Palace" of white-painted glass is the oldest building in *Golden Gate Park*. Originally intended for the grounds of a San Jose mansion, the Victorian structure was erected in 1879 in the park as the first municipal greenhouse. Temperature and humidity are exact in this specialized growing environment. One section of the conservatory displays tropical plants, with a wide variety of orchids (which are considered endangered species), including the only public display of Masdevallia and Dracula orchids in North America. Colorful hibiscus and unusual-looking bromeliads are exhibited as well. Another wing features huge seasonal displays of flowering plants in all their colorful variations. Tropical water lilies and Egyptian lotus grow and bloom in two indoor ponds. More than 4,000 plants are maintained in the conservatory collection. Open daily; admission charge. Information: *Conservatory of Flowers,* John F. Kennedy Dr. (no phone).

JAPANESE TEA GARDEN This serene five-acre garden is a jewel in this huge park. Winding paths lead past a large bronze Buddha; the Moon Bridge casts its shadow on the surface of a pond to create the image of a complete circle; cherry trees bloom profusely in spring. Benches are strategically placed so that visitors can enjoy the many tranquil settings. Built as a Japanese village for the 1894 *California Midwinter International Exposition* in *Golden Gate Park,* the gardens were carefully planned and tended by Japanese landscape gardener Makoto Hagiwara. Jasmine tea and cookies are served in the *Tea Pavilion* in the center of the garden. Open daily; admission charge. Information: *Japanese Tea Garden,* Hagiwara Tea Garden Dr. (phone: 415-752-4227).

STRYBING ARBORETUM AND BOTANICAL GARDENS More than 6,000 species of plants grow in this 70-acre area of *Golden Gate Park*. A lake near the center of the arboretum attracts ducks and migrating birds. Circular pathways divide the planting areas into subsections devoted to the flora of different climatic regions. A fragrance garden, with plants of strong scents and unusual textures, has braille labels. Native California plants landscape one loop; another garden showcases plants mentioned in the Bible. Guides are sold in the arboretum shop; an annual flower show takes place each August in the *Hall of Flowers*. Open daily with free tours available; no admission charge. Information: *Strybing Arboretum,* Martin Luther King Jr. Dr. (phone: 415-661-1316).

Visitable Vineyards

Whether you're in search of the perfect cabernet or the perfect vacation, you'll find it in California's wine country. A dozen years ago, you might have flown to Europe. Today California wines are grabbing gold medals in blind tastings against the finest French bordeaux, burgundies, and many others, and winery touring is one of the newest American pursuits.

VINTAGE ROUTES

America's wine capitals are the Napa and Sonoma Valleys, with more than 200 wineries open to the public within a one or two hours' drive of San Francisco. For those who would like an extended visit, the *Auberge du Soleil* (180 Rutherford Hill Rd., Rutherford, CA 94573; phone: 707-963-1211 or 800-348-5406); *Meadowood Resort* (900 Meadowood La., St. Helena, CA 94574; phone: 707-963-3646 or 800-458-8080); and *Sonoma Mission Inn & Spa* (PO Box 1447, Sonoma, CA 95476 or 18140 Sonoma Hwy. 12, Boyes Hot Springs, CA 95416; phone: 707-938-9000 or 800-358-9022) offer elegant accommodations and tours of the wine country. For more information on Napa lodging, call *Wine Country Reservations* at 707-257-7757.

What makes wine touring the ideal travel diversion is the vine's own finicky nature. Grapes thrive in protected valleys and on gentle hillsides warmed by long hours of sunshine and cooled by ocean breezes that are dream settings for day-trippers and vacationers, as well as serious oenophiles.

Furthermore, vintners—from the giant conglomerate to the lone maker in a four-car garage—are anxious to showcase their products. At small wineries you'll probably be taken through by the owner, who'll taste with you and share production secrets down to the last barrel stave. These visits require planning, since appointments usually must be made in advance. For more casual visits try larger wineries with tasting rooms open to drop-ins. They're apt to be better organized for touring the vineyards, the crushing pads, and the fermentation rooms, with their giant steel tanks, endless rows of aging barrels, and clattering bottling lines.

Tastings of current wines usually are complimentary (like the tours), though a few big houses have started to charge admission. Some wineries pour grape juice for children and for whomever is driving. Start with the whites and work your way up through the full-bodied reds to the sweet dessert wines. Don't hesitate to "chew" the wine, swishing it around in your mouth and then spitting it out (as professional tasters do), or to empty unconsumed wine from your glass into the crocks set along the tasting bar.

Bus trips sometimes are offered out of San Francisco, but generally you'll need a car for wine touring. Bring low-heel, rubber-sole shoes for climbing up observation ramps and stepping over hoses on wet floors. Bring a sweater, too, for chilly, damp aging cellars. Since many wineries are open only from around 10 AM to 4 PM, and there may be a wait for tours, don't plan more than four stops a day. If you drive, time your visit for spring if you want to avoid the July-through-September vacation crowds and the October weekend stampedes. With autumn's arrival, the tempo quickens, the grapes hang heavy, and the trucks line up to dump their gleaming harvest onto the crushing pads. If you come in summer, you'll face bumper-to-bumper traffic and crowds jostling for places at the tasting bar, unless you stay in San Francisco on the weekend and visit Napa midweek. Note that although many vineyards are open daily to visitors, almost all are closed on major holidays, and the majority offer their tours for no charge; call to check.

Though there are pockets of scenic wine country from Mendocino County, well to the north of San Francisco, all the way down to the Mexican border, the ultimate—and most accessible—are super-chic Napa Valley and gentrified Sonoma County. These premium grape-growing areas, home to megabuck international wine companies and millionaire "farmers," serve up a trendy vacation lifestyle with calculated rusticity. Napa Valley's *Oakville Grocery Company* (7856 St. Helena Hwy., Oakville; phone: 707-944-8802) sells picnic pâtés and cheeses worthy of *Fauchon* in Paris. At the *Downtown Bakery and Creamery* (308-A Center St.; phone: 707-431-2719), on the sleepy little Healdsburg town square in Sonoma County, the croissants are turned out by the pastry chef of Berkeley's well-known *Chez Panisse* restaurant. Its homemade ice cream is also superb.

For general information on California wines, contact the *Wine Institute* (425 Market St., Suite 1000, San Francisco, CA 94105; phone: 415-512-0151).

NAPA VALLEY

Some 30 miles long and 6 miles across at its widest point, cozy Napa Valley, with 25,000 acres of micro-climates and soil variations at every turn, is the promised land for cabernet sauvignon, pinot noir, chardonnay, sauvignon blanc, Johannisberg riesling, and many more of the world's finest grape varieties. It's also a playground for winery touring, ballooning, cycling, hiking, picnicking, boutiquing, fine dining, and discovering charming inns. Its main road, Highway 29, runs the length of the valley, chockablock with vineyards and wineries, and winds through the gussied-up country towns of Napa, Yountville, St. Helena, and Calistoga, which soon become as familiar as your own hometown.

Napa is one of California's biggest tourist attractions—so big that there's now a *Wine Train* that makes the 36-mile round trip, offering luncheon and dinner excursions and champagne brunch trips on weekends aboard elegant 1915-vintage Pullman parlor cars (1275 McKinstry St., Napa, CA 94559; phone: 707-253-2111 or 800-522-4142 for reservations).

Here's a sample of the range of experiences you'll find in Napa's wineries.

BERINGER It's hard to miss this turreted Rhineland mansion from the road. Stop at its lavish, paneled tasting rooms and take the fascinating tour of hand-dug caves still showing the pick-ax marks left by Chinese laborers in the 1870s. Beringer doesn't make its wines right here, but there's a lot to see. Open daily for tours. Information: *Beringer Vineyards,* 2000 Main St., PO Box 111, St. Helena, CA 94574 (phone: 707-963-7115).

CHÂTEAU MONTELENA You have to ask the way to this century-old stone palace shrouded by woods at the north end of the valley. After a tour and tasting, visitors can purchase a bottle of its famous chardonnay or cabernet and picnic among the black swans on the island in the château's pond. Picnic and tour reservations are required, but the tasting room is always open; there's an admission charge. Information: *Château Montelena*, 1429 Tubbs La., Calistoga, CA 94515 (phone: 707-942-5105).

CLOS PEGASE Designed by the famous postmodern architect Michael Graves, this ocher-and-rust-colored, many-columned complex has been described as a cross between a nuclear reactor and a Greek temple. The winery tour, not surprisingly, devotes as much attention to architectural detail as to the process of making chardonnay and fumé blanc. The tasting room is open daily; tours by appointment only. Information: *Clos Pegase*, 1060 Dunaweal La., PO Box 305, Calistoga, CA 94515 (phone: 707-942-4981).

CLOS DU VAL This unpretentious modern French château faces Napa's Silverado Trail, the road that runs along the quieter, eastern edge of the valley, where pasturelands evoke a time when Napa was dairy country. In the vineyards that lead up from the road, a rose bush has been planted (a French custom) at the end of each row of vines. Tours are by appointment, and you can taste a range of outstanding varietals, including uniquely Californian zinfandel. Information: *Clos du Val Wine Company*, 5330 Silverado Trail, PO Box 4350, Napa, CA 94558 (phone: 707-252-6711).

CODORNIU NAPA Approached by climbing steps past waterfalls and reflecting pools, this hillside winery (owned by the Codorniu family of Spain) affords breathtaking panoramic views of the Carneros region. Tours are offered daily. Sparkling wine may be purchased for sampling inside or out on the patio. Open daily. Take Highway 101 to the Napa Valley exit; follow this road (Hwy. 37) 12 miles to Old Sonoma Highway; exit at Dealy Lane and go north for 1.6 miles to Henry Road. Information: *Codorniu Napa*, 1345 Henry Rd., Napa, CA 94558 (phone: 707-224-1668).

DOMAINE CARNEROS This imposing $13-million facility was modeled after Taittinger's 18th-century château in Reims, France. Tours are free; there's a charge for a glass of sparkling wine with an hors d'oeuvre. Open daily, June through October; Fridays through Tuesdays, November through May. Located on Highway 12/121 between the Napa and Sonoma Valleys. Information: *Domaine Carneros*, 1240 Duhig Rd., Napa, CA 94581 (phone: 707-257-0101).

DOMAINE CHANDON Seeming to grow out of the earth, this low-slung symphony of stone arches looks out across a valley of vines to the golden, oak-studded hills on the other side. Tours of this arm of the glamorous French firm Moët et Chandon begin in an underground wine museum and proceed through a high-production sparkling wine–making operation. You'll see the unusual sight of high fermentation tanks lying on their sides and inspect the latest automatic riddling machines (for periodic turning of the bottles).

There's no tasting with this tour, but you can buy a glass of bubbly (try the réserve) in a sunny sit-down café. Open daily, Wednesdays through Sundays. *Domaine Chandon* also has an internationally known restaurant serving lunch and dinner, which requires reservations well in advance. Information: *Domaine Chandon,* California Dr., PO Box 2470, Yountville, CA 94599 (phone: 707-944-2280).

FLORA SPRINGS This is a real family business, whose owners will show you how they saved and updated an ancient winery. Bring barbecue fixings and use the grill on their hilltop picnic patio. By appointment only. Information: *Flora Springs Wine Co.,* 1978 W. Zinfandel La., St. Helena, CA 95474 (phone: 707-963-5711).

GRGICH HILLS Connoisseurs come to this attractive hacienda for its whites, particularly the handsome chardonnays. The tasting room welcomes drop-in visitors, but tours are by appointment. Open daily. Information: *Grgich Hills Cellar,* 1829 St. Helena Hwy. (Hwy.29), PO Box 450, Rutherford, CA 94573 (phone: 707-963-2784).

HESS COLLECTION Though his gallery/winery is located off the beaten path, Swiss-American art collector/winery owner Donald Hess shares his 130-piece collection of works by contemporary artists such as Robert Motherwell, Frank Stella, and the late Francis Bacon, to name a few. Self-guided tours include the art and the winery (mostly chardonnay and cabernet sauvignon). Open daily; there is a charge for tasting. Information: *The Hess Collection,* 4411 Redwood Rd., PO Box 4140, Napa, CA 94558 (phone: 707-255-1144).

INGLENOOK Inside a historic stone building dating back to 1879, a 10-minute film provides a great visual overview of how grapes grow and the process that turns them into wine; the winery also boasts a collection of photographs and artifacts on the history of wine making in the Napa Valley. Corporate-owned and -operated its wine is no longer made on the premises. Open daily, but occasionally closes for private events. First tours are at 11 AM weekdays, 10:30 AM weekends. Information: *Inglenook Vineyards,* 1991 St. Helena Hwy. (Hwy. 29), PO Box 19, Rutherford, CA 94573 (phone: 707-967-3358).

MONTICELLO CELLARS People come to see the property patterned after Thomas Jefferson's Virginia home, but you should also taste the well-made wines; picnicking is possible on the grounds. Open daily; tour hours vary (call ahead for reservations). Information: *Monticello Cellars,* 4242 Big Ranch Rd., Napa, CA 94558 (phone: 707-253-2802).

MUMM NAPA VALLEY This local *méthode champenoise* producer offers a daily tour program that provides a distinctive taste of sparkling wine making. Guided tours are offered daily; visitors may purchase wine by the glass or by the bottle to sip leisurely while nibbling complimentary hors d'oeuvres on the large porch, which overlooks the vineyards and the Mayacamas Mountains.

Information: *Mumm Napa Valley,* 8445 Silverado Trail, Napa, CA 94558 (phone: 800-686-6272).

PRAGER In a two-story wood-frame winery building off the main highway, a dedicated vintner is championing a port revival. His modest output is available on the premises—in bottles personally autographed in gold ink. His tasting room is the kitchen behind a minuscule barrel room. Tasting and tours by appointment only. There are also two bed and breakfast suites here. Information: *Prager Winery & Port Works,* 1281 Lewelling La., St. Helena, CA 94574 (phone: 707-963-PORT; 707-963-3720 for bed and breakfast reservations).

ROBERT MONDAVI The best guided tour in the valley is at this white, V-shaped, mission-style winery surrounded by flower gardens. There's a dramatic view of the vineyards, framed by an entrance archway, where a statue of St. Francis stands guard. Tours paced with the precision of a TV game show give comprehensive walk-throughs from vineyard to bottling and end with a tasting that's a learning experience; there's also a summer jazz series. Tours are offered daily in summer; reservations (by phone) are strongly recommended. Information: *Robert Mondavi Winery,* 7801 St. Helena Hwy., PO Box 106, Oakville, CA 94562 (phone: 707-963-9611).

STERLING When locals grumble about the Disneyfication of Napa, they point to the wildly popular white ski gondolas that lift visitors from the parking lot to the white building of this imposing winery, which was modeled after a hilltop monastery in Greece. Once aloft, you get breathtaking views downvalley; a well-organized self-guided tour (follow the signs) along ramps overlooking the works follows. Included in the gondola fee is a sit-down tasting of cabernets, chardonnays, pinot noirs, sauvignon blancs, and merlots in a luxurious tower room. Open daily. Information: *Sterling Vineyards,* 1111 Dunaweal La., PO Box 365, Calistoga, CA 94515 (phone: 707-942-5151).

SONOMA COUNTY

Just over the mountains, less than a half hour west of the Napa Valley, lies a more spread out, slightly cooler wine country. It offers rural calm, uncrowded roads, plentiful accommodations, and a chance to soak up California history. The Sonoma town square, for instance, was the site of the Bear Flag uprising in 1823 that declared California's independence from Mexico. Sonoma County's closely linked wine valleys—Alexander, Dry Creek, Sonoma, and Russian River—still have room for pear and apple orchards, truck farms, horse ranches, a dairy, and farms among the vineyards. There's even an organized "farm route" that leads to farm stands, llama- and pony-petting corrals, and cheese- and jam-making enterprises that offer a good break between wineries—ideal if you're touring with children. The *Sonoma County Wineries Association* has a visitors' center (5000 Roberts Lake Rd., Rohnert Park; phone: 707-586-3795) that features an interactive video terminal to help plan a tour of area wineries, a facsimile of a winery, and a wine-tasting bar. And a few companies offer tours of the wine country by horse-drawn carriage, often with picnics ranging from chuck wagon–style to finer fare. *Wine Country Carriages* (3325 Gravenstein Hwy. N., Sebastopol, CA 95472; phone: 707-823-7083) takes visitors through the wine country in turn-of-the-century, horse-drawn conveyances; depending upon the season, stops are made at *Christmas* tree and berry farms and apple orchards as well. *Wine Country Wagons* (PO Box 1069, Kenwood, CA 95452; phone: 707-833-2724) offers trips to several wineries and ends with a picnic lunch at a private ranch. Trips usually are scheduled in the spring and run through October.

BENZIGER FAMILY WINERY This is the former *Glen Ellen Winery and Vineyards.* Down the hill from historic *Jack London State Park* near the tiny crossroads town of Glen Ellen, a cluster of modest white, frame buildings snuggles in a hollow that looks up at a patchwork quilt of terraced vineyards. Instead of taking a formal tour, browse among the vineyards, tanks, and barrels yourself, and ask questions in the tasting room. A towering grove of redwoods shading the picnic grounds is a reminder that you're at the edge of California's redwood country. Open daily; tours at 11 AM and 2 PM. Information: *Benziger Family Winery,* 1883 London Ranch Rd., Glen Ellen, CA 95442 (phone: 707-935-3000).

BUENA VISTA This is a state historic landmark rather than a working vineyard. A short drive into the hills from Sonoma leads to the place where scoundrel/adventurer Agoston Haraszthy planted the first European wine grapes in California in 1857. The romantic ivy-covered stone buildings house an art gallery and a wine museum; the fine Buena Vista wines tasted here are made at another location. There's picnicking under giant eucalyptus trees along the stream out front. Open daily, with a presentation each day at 2 PM on the history of the site and of winemaking in the region. Information: *Buena Vista Winery and Tasting Room,* 18000 Old Winery Rd., PO Box 1842, Sonoma, CA 95476 (phone: 707-938-1266 or 800-926-1266).

CHÂTEAU ST. JEAN Take a self-guided tour through a Mediterranean-style winery building set well back in the vineyards, and look out over the Sonoma Valley from the winery's tower. Taste its premium whites in a charming villa across a flower-filled courtyard. Open daily. Information: *Château St. Jean,* 8555 Sonoma Hwy., PO Box 293, Kenwood, CA 95452 (phone: 707-833-4134).

CHÂTEAU SOUVERAIN Here is a most impressive winery building set on an Alexander Valley hillside. Enjoy tastings plus outstanding dining-with-a-view, at moderate prices, at lunch or dinner. Open Thursdays through Mondays. Information: *Château Souverain,* Independence La., PO Box 528, Geyserville, CA 95441 (phone: 707-433-8281).

FERRARI-CARANO This Italianate winery is surrounded by vineyards and five acres of manicured lawns bordered by Old World rock and flower gardens. Stop by for tastings, which include a popular chardonnay. Tours of the shiny facilities can be arranged by appointment. Information: *Ferrari-Carano Vineyards & Winery,* 8761 Dry Creek Rd., PO Box 1549, Healdsburg, CA 95448 (phone: 707-433-6700).

GLORIA FERRER CHAMPAGNE CAVES This offshoot of Spain's *Freixenet* winery offers informative tours through its lavish Catalonian-contemporary complex, with panoramic views of Sonoma County from the wine-bar terrace. Tours (free) and tastings (charge) are offered daily. Information: *Gloria Ferrer Champagne Caves,* 23555 Hwy. 121, PO Box 1949, Sonoma, CA 95476 (phone: 707-996-7256).

HANNA There's an attractive tasting room at this winery founded by San Francisco heart surgeon Elias Hanna. The best successes here have been with sauvignon blanc and chardonnay. Open weekdays only. Information: *Hanna Winery,* 5345 Occidental Rd., Santa Rosa, CA 95406 (phone: 707-575-3330).

HOP KILN Located on a state historic landmark site, this moldering stone building out in the country provides a look back to the days before the wine boom, when Sonoma's vineyards were hop fields for a thriving beer industry. The building's three square towers actually are chimneys for the old hop-drying furnaces that stand alongside the wine-making tanks and barrels. There are no tours, but there are daily tastings throughout the day. Try the zinfandel. Information: *Hop Kiln Winery,* 6050 Westside Rd., Healdsburg, CA 95448 (phone: 707-433-6491).

IRON HORSE Call ahead to enjoy the understated elegance of this privately owned estate winery on its own hilltop, reached by a narrow, rutted road. Surrounded by vine-covered hills that shut out the world, you'll stroll through the property, a glass of sparkling wine in hand, as a winemaker shows you around. You'll be given more tastes of cabernet, chardonnay, and fumé blanc in a barrel-aging room. Tour and tasting by appointment only. Lunch in the gazebo is a little bit of wine country heaven. Information: *Iron Horse Vineyards,* 9786 Ross Station Rd., Sebastopol, CA 95472 (phone: 707-887-1507).

KORBEL The biggest champagne maker in the US conducts one of the most thorough guided tours, ending with a generous free tasting at a block-long bar made from old barrels. There are also tours of the impressive gardens with plants from all over the world, Tuesdays through Saturdays at 11 AM and 3 PM only. Founded in 1882 near the Russian River, Korbel has its original buildings in place, within a grove of antique roses. Vineyard tours are offered daily. Information: *Korbel Champagne Cellars,* 13250 River Rd., Guerneville, CA 95446 (phone: 707-887-2294).

SEBASTIANI There's constant hubbub in the tasting room–gift shop of this winery, which has operated in the town of Sonoma since 1904. The giant vineyards produce more than a dozen varieties for tasting. Daily tours are well guided and include a look at a fascinating collection of hand-carved casks. Information: *Sebastiani Vineyards,* 389 Fourth St. E., PO Box AA, Sonoma, CA 95476 (phone: 707-938-5532).

VIANSA This luxurious Tuscan-style hillside villa brings the charm of the Italian wine country to California. Surrounded by a grove of olive trees, it has beautiful hand-painted murals and frescoes, stone fermentation tanks, and a vaulted cellar. The winery also has its own kitchen, where fresh food is prepared daily using "Cal-Ital" recipes. Sip the superb wine and eat at picnic tables, which afford a stunning view of the valley. The owners are members of the pioneer Sebastiani wine-making family. Tours are given daily. Information: *Viansa Winery,* 25200 Arnold Dr. (Hwy. 121), Sonoma, CA 95476 (phone: 707-935-4700).

JUST FOR THE TASTE OF IT

Sampling the extraordinary quality and variety of wines produced by California's vintners does not require a journey beyond the city limits of San Francisco. Several good wine shops have tasting bars and many boast an impressive collection of bottles from small local producers. Wines from these "boutique" wineries are often hard to come by outside the Bay Area. Anyone with an interest in or knowledge of wine will enjoy browsing, and maybe even buying, at any one of the following establishments.

Draper & Esquin (655 Davis St., near the *Embarcadero Center;* phone: 415-397-3797) has an excellent selection of rare, imported, and California wines. Older vintages as well as bottles from small California vineyards also can be found here. The *Pacific Wine Co.* (124 Spear St., across from *Rincon Center;* phone: 415-896-5200) specializes in bordeaux, burgundy, champagne, and Rhône wines, along with a good sampling from the smaller California vineyards. The shop has a small tasting bar. A wine bar with an extensive daily tasting list, *Wine Impression* (3461 California St.; phone: 415-221-9463), carries a large selection of mature and moderately aged wines. Some older vintages sold here actually appeared on the wine list of the *Palace* hotel (now the *Sheraton Palace*) in 1906. The *London Wine Bar* (415 Sansome St.; phone: 415-788-4811), which claims the distinction of being America's first wine bar, offers what is probably the best selection of wine-by-the-glass anywhere: On any given day about 30 different wines can be sampled. Lunch and appetizers also are served here, and the restaurant has a retail license, so you can buy a bottle to go.

The Great Outdoors

If you're set for sailing, ready to run, hooked on hiking, revved up for rollerblading, or just like having your head in the clouds, here are some ways to relish San Francisco outdoors.

SAILING ON THE BAY Anyone can be a sailor out on San Francisco Bay, racing with the wind at your back and the spray in your eyes. From a ketch or a sloop, views from the water are unparalleled. But wise sailors are not fooled by the word "bay." The water can be rough, the winds wild, and the underwater topography unpredictable. Adding heavy boat traffic and sudden fog, sailing the bay can be challenging. *A Day on the Bay* (Gate 10, *San Francisco Marina;* Buchanan St. and Marina Blvd.; phone: 415-922-0227) rents sailboats to experienced sailors, or you can hire a skipper for the boat you take out. Ketches, sloops, and yawls—from 20 to 64 feet—are well maintained and available by the hour. Would-be sailors can arrange for a day of lessons. Boats come without provisions; stow away a movable feast. *A Day on the Bay* accepts out-of-state checks but not credit cards; reservations required.

THAR THEY BLOW!

Whale watchers and fanciers of other denizens of the deep can get up close during a day cruise to the Farallon Islands offered by *Oceanic Society Expeditions* (*Fort Mason Center,* Bldg. E; phone: 415-474-3385). Rocky outcroppings 27 miles west of the city, the Farallons afford visitors intimate views of sea mammals in their natural habitat. In addition to Moby Dick's mob, island residents—or at least those who pass by—include dolphins, porpoises, sea lions, and seals, plus nearly 200,000 seabirds—puffins, auklets, cormorants, and albatross, to name just a few. Members of *Friends of the Earth,* an environmental advocacy group, discuss the history and preservation of the creatures. Wildlife cruises sail on weekends from June through November; whale-watching cruises run from late December through April. Reservations are essential.

WINDSURFING What Huntington, Malibu, and Rincon were to the *Beach Boys* generation, Maui, Hood River, and San Francisco are to today's windsurfers. Maui has the waves, Hood the velocity, and San Francisco, from May to September, the dependability. The premier spot here is off *Crissy Field* in the *Presidio,* with the tiny armada skittering around oceangoing freighters and tankers. Morning beginner classes, conducted in the more sheltered waters of Lake Merced on the south edge of the city, last two days. For information, contact the *San Francisco School of Windsurfing,* 1 Harding Rd. (phone: 415-750-0412).

ROAD RUNNERS Climbing up and down hills all day long may not constitute exercise for serious joggers, who need to feel their feet pounding rhythmically over the pavement for the movement really to count. Running is serious business in San Francisco, and aside from the hilly terrain, there are ample stretches of level ground right along some of the most beautiful places in the city. The *Marina Green* is a popular starting point. Head west and follow the shoreline through the *Presidio's Crissy Field* to the base of the *Golden Gate Bridge,* with its sweeping views of the bay. Or, head east, past *Fort Mason, Fisherman's Wharf,* and *Pier 39,* to the broad walkway of *The Embarcadero* and the silver shimmer of the San Francisco–Oakland Bay Bridge.

Golden Gate Park is another popular alternative. On Sundays some roads through the park are closed to vehicles, giving joggers even more freedom. And just jogging through a neighborhood can offer a different perspective on the city's architecture and ethnic diversity.

Even with a sport as simple as running, San Franciscans inject their own form of zaniness once a year, when world class runners take to the same field as world class nuts for the *Bay to Breakers* run. Billed as the world's largest foot race, this annual May event has been run for over 80 consecutive years. Part *Halloween,* part *Mardi Gras,* this is an entertaining event even for those who have no interest in the sport. Starting at Howard and Spear Streets at the foot of the Bay Bridge, and running through the financial district and the western addition to *Golden Gate Park* and out to the ocean, an elite flight of internationally known runners race 7.5 miles (12 km) alongside joggers dressed as broccoli, TV characters, and famous politicians. In recent years more than 100,000 participants have taken to the streets for each annual run. Centipedes are one favorite participatory formation; students of a chiropractic school run together in a line, each costumed as one part of a spine; friends and coworkers outfit themselves as the *Rockettes* or a cable car. To register, send a self-addressed, stamped business envelope to *Examiner Bay to Breakers,* PO Box 42000, San Francisco, CA 94142. For additional information, call the *San Francisco Examiner* at 415-777-7773.

HIKING The great outdoors is everywhere in and around San Francisco, and people make good use of it. Portions of the city's northern and western waterfront—and the entire 1,400-acre *Presidio,* formerly an Army base—are included in the *Golden Gate National Recreation Area,* which spans three counties and almost 73,000 acres. In San Francisco hiking trails wind through the *Presidio* to *Fort Point National Historic Site,* a 19th-century coastal fortification. Lands End is a favorite in-city retreat from the day-to-day pressures of urban existence: Along the rocky cliffs the crashing ocean obscures the sounds of cars and buses, but not the twittering of birds, and the limbs of cypress and pine trees stretch up to create a more natural skyline.

Just across the bay the Marin Headlands rise from the water on the northern side of the *Golden Gate Bridge*. Hiking trails run across the ridges and through the valleys, offering glorious views of San Francisco and the shimmering Pacific Ocean, and close-ups of the region's flora and fauna. Pack drinking water and food—amenities here are few and far between. Detailed trail maps are available at ranger stations. For information on the Headlands, call 415-331-1540.

For more serious hikers, there's *Mt. Tamalpais State Park*. Rising 2,600 feet above sea level, Mt. Tamalpais (known affectionately as "Mt. Tam") is a favorite among hard-core trekkers. Muir Woods, the only virgin stand of redwood trees in Marin County, is a popular attraction, but most visitors never venture beyond its borders to explore the reservoirs and trails that wind over and around the mountain. From the summit loop trail on a crisp, clear day, hikers can see as far away as 200 miles, to the Sierra Nevadas. Wildflowers bloom profusely in the spring, and hundreds of species of birds live among the varied plant communities that thrive here. For those who prefer to explore nature in the company of a group and a guide, hikes, bird watching, and other expeditions are listed each Monday in the "Outings" section of the *San Francisco Chronicle*. *Golden Gate Transit* buses connect the city with Marin hiking outposts on weekends and holidays (phone: 415-332-6600). Spartan, popular cabins overlook the ocean at Steep Ravine (phone: 800-444-7275). For park information, call 415-388-2070.

HANG GLIDING Almost everyone has a grandmother or aunt or friend who says it: People in San Francisco are crazy. If you've ever fantasized about jumping off cliffs and flying through the air, then this is the perfect place to live out that fantasy. The *Chandelle Hang Gliding Center* (6880 Sir Francis Drake Blvd., Forest Knolls; 30 minutes north of the *Golden Gate Bridge;* phone: 415-488-4202) offers a four- to six-hour session with hang gliding or paragliding lessons and equipment. "Put wings on your dreams," urge the instructors. Or, if you're not up for the challenge yourself, head down to *Fort Funston* (just south of the *San Francisco Zoo* on Highway 35) and watch the daring young fliers. *Chandelle* is open Saturdays and weekday afternoons except Wednesdays.

A Shutterbug's San Francisco

If you can get it to hold still long enough, San Francisco is an exceptionally photogenic city. There is architectural variety: Victorian houses nestle up to Art Deco apartment buildings; a skyline of rectangular skyscrapers is punctuated by a pyramid-shape tower and the arched, mirrored façade of a hotel; old is juxtaposed with new. There is natural variety: Giant redwood trees soar between manmade architectural feats; gingko trees—the plant world's link between prehistoric ferns and modern trees—shade the sidewalk in front of a Gold Rush–era brick bank building; flowers reach out of their containers along steep steps climbing ever uphill. There's human variety as well: Shoppers in Chinatown bargain with merchants in rapid-fire Cantonese; ruddy fishermen return with their catch at the same piers where tourists sort through sweatshirts and seashells; stocky sports fans sit cheek-by-jowl dressed in their team's full regalia. The thriving city, the shimmering bay, the parks, the people, and traces of rich history make San Francisco a fertile stomping ground for shutterbugs. Even a beginner can achieve remarkable results with a surprisingly basic set of lenses and filters. Equipment is, in fact, only as valuable as the imagination that puts it into use.

LANDSCAPES, SEASCAPES, AND CITYSCAPES San Francisco's Victorian houses and historic cable cars, elegant bridges, and colorful waterfront are most often visiting photographers' favorite subjects. But the city's green spaces and hidden alleys provide numerous photo possibilities as well. In addition to *Misión Dolores,* the *Ferry Building,* and *Coit Tower,* be sure to look for natural beauty: prehistoric-looking tree ferns in *Golden Gate Park;* a parade of brightly colored spinnakers on sailboats crisscrossing the bay; the small, well-manicured gardens of Pacific Heights; and the tree-lined lagoon reflecting the Greek and Roman lines of the *Palace of Fine Arts* are just a few examples.

Although a standard 50mm to 55mm lens may work well in some landscape situations, most will benefit from a 20mm to 28mm wide-angle. The colorfully painted Victorians along Alamo Square, with city skyscrapers looming in the distance, for example, is the type of panorama that fits beautifully into a wide-angle format, allowing not only the overview, but the opportunity to include people or other points of interest in the foreground. A flower, for instance, may be used to set off a view of *Coit Tower;* or people can provide a sense of perspective in a shot along the Golden Gate Promenade.

To isolate specific elements of any scene, use your telephoto lens. Perhaps there's a particular carving on a California Street bank that would make a lovely shot, or it might be the interplay of light and shadow in the gardens that line the Filbert Street steps. The successful use of a telephoto means developing your eye for detail.

PEOPLE As with taking pictures of people anywhere, there are going to be times in San Francisco when a camera is an intrusion. Consider your own reaction under similar circumstances, and you have an idea as to what would make others comfortable enough to be willing subjects. People are often sensitive to having a camera suddenly thrust at them, but a polite request, while getting you a share of refusals, will also provide a chance to shoot some wonderful portraits that capture the spirit of the city as surely as the scenery does. For candids an excellent lens is a zoom telephoto in the 70mm to 210mm range; it allows you to remain unobtrusive while the lens draws the subject closer. And for portraits a telephoto can be used effectively from as close as two or three feet.

For authenticity and variety select a place likely to produce interesting subjects. *Fisherman's Wharf* is an obvious spot for visitors, but if it's local color you're after, visit Chinatown or stroll along 24th Street in the mission district; sit at a Haight-Ashbury café and watch the parade of punk and retro-hippie fashions; or walk through *Golden Gate Park,* where the young and old, the well-heeled and the down-at-the-heels flock to enjoy a sunny day. Aim for shots that portray what's different about San Francisco. In portraiture there are several factors to keep in mind. Morning or afternoon light will add richness to skin tones, emphasizing tans. To avoid the harsh facial shadows cast by direct sunlight, shoot in the shade or in an area where the light is diffused.

SUNSETS When shooting sunsets, keep in mind that the brightness will distort meter readings. When composing a shot directly into the sun, frame the picture in the viewfinder so that only half of the sun is included. Read the meter, set, and shoot. Whenever there is this kind of unusual lighting, shoot a few frames in half-step increments, both over and under the meter reading. Bracketing, as this is called, can provide a range of images, the best of which may well be other than the one shot at the meter's recommended setting.

Use any lens for sunsets. A wide-angle is good when the sky is filled with color-streaked clouds, when the sun is partially hidden, or when you're close to an object that silhouettes dramatically against the sky.

Telephotos also produce wonderful silhouettes, either with the sun as a backdrop or against the palette of a brilliant sunset sky. Bracket again here. For the best silhouettes wait 10 to 15 minutes after sunset. Unless using a very fast film, a tripod is recommended.

Red and orange filters are often used to accentuate a sunset's picture potential. Orange will help turn even a gray sky into something approaching a photogenic finale to the day, and can provide particularly beautiful shots linking the sky with the sun reflected on the ocean. If the sunset is already bold in hue, however, the orange will overwhelm natural colors. A red filter will produce dramatic but highly unrealistic results.

NIGHT If you think that picture possibilities end at sunset, you're presuming that night photography is the exclusive domain of the professional. If you've got a tripod, all you'll need is a cable release to attach to your camera to assure a steady exposure (which is often timed in minutes, rather than fractions of a second).

For situations such as nighttime bay cruises, a strobe does the trick, but beware: Flash units are often used improperly. You can't take a view of the skyline with a flash. It may reach out as far as 30 feet, but that's it. On the other hand a flash used too close to a subject may result in overexposure, resulting in a "blown-out" effect. With most cameras strobes will work with a maximum shutter speed of 1/125 or 1/250 of a second. If you set the exposure properly and shoot within range, you should come up with pretty sharp results.

CLOSE-UPS Whether of people or of objects such as antique door knockers, close-ups can add another dimension to your photography. There are a number of shooting options, one of which is to use a 70mm or a 210mm lens at its closest focusable distance. Unless you're working in bright sunlight, a tripod will be worthwhile. If you are very near your subject and there is a good deal of reflective light, it may pay to underexpose a bit in relation to the meter reading.

If you do not have a telephoto lens, you can still shoot close-ups using a set of magnification filters. Filter packs of one-, two-, and three-time magnification are available, converting your regular lens into a close-up lens. Even better is a special macro lens designed for close-up photography.

A SHORT PHOTOGRAPHIC TOUR

Here are some of San Francisco's truly great pictorial perspectives.

GHIRARDELLI SQUARE The best vantage point for the perfect picture of *Ghirardelli Square* is out in the bay—attainable without a boat by walking to the end of the municipal pier at the foot of Van Ness Avenue. *Ghirardelli*'s red and yellow brick towers—the former site of a chocolate factory with roots dating back to the Gold Rush era—form the center of the picture, crowned by the chocolate company's famous electric sign. Downhill (and in the foreground) the dazzling white *National Maritime Museum* sits snugly at the edge of *Aquatic Park,* mirroring the shape of the vessels tied up in the cove; uphill (and in the background) high-rise buildings lay claim to more contemporary history. Late afternoon and early evening are good times to capture *Ghirardelli Square,* when the sign is lighted and stands out against the sky.

PALACE OF FINE ARTS Standing near the intersection of Baker and Beach Streets are the rose and golden rotunda and colonnade of Bernard Maybeck's *Palace of Fine Arts.* Frame the shot with the soft burgundy and green leaves of the dense growth of trees here, and be sure to aim high enough to capture the "Weeping Ladies" that grace the top of each section along the colonnade. White sea gulls resting on the water's surface add a touch of brightness in the foreground.

PAINTED LADIES Another favorite view of San Francisco is the well-known "Painted Ladies," the Victorian houses that line Alamo Square. Most impressive is the juxtaposition of these well-maintained 19th-century residences to the cityscape beyond—high-rises, hills, and the Transamerica Pyramid. For the best picture stand on Hayes Street, between Steiner and Pierce, looking east toward Steiner—from this hillside, old and new blend together. Like Monet's series of Impressionist paintings of the *Rouen Cathedral,* the results will be different at different times of day; even a low-lying bank of fog can add another dimension to this picture.

HYDE STREET CABLE CAR LINE Much of what you might want to remember about San Francisco can be recorded in this one photograph. Stand on the western side of Hyde Street, at the corner of Chestnut, and wait for a cable car to come rattling down the hill, making its descent to the waterfront. Snap the picture as it passes, just as it breaks the crest of the hill (it will give the illusion of flying over the edge—the street below is not visible). From this angle, Alcatraz is sharp and clear in the shimmering blue bay; the bluffs of Angel Island are less focused in the background. Trees and architecturally interesting buildings line Hyde Street—the quintessential elements needed to preserve memories of a visit to San Francisco.

FERRY BUILDING Walk all the way to the end of Pier 7 for a remarkable view of the historic *Ferry Building* (built in 1896), which sits squarely at the eastern end of Market Street. From this angle (which is almost like being on a boat), the "Port of San Francisco" sign is legible, as are the familiar gold dome and the American flag, battered by the constant breeze. The very regular pattern of rectangular windows on the tall buildings of the financial district provide a nice counterpoint to this cathedral-inspired tower.

GOLDEN GATE BRIDGE Walk to the end of the path at Battery Spencer in the Marin Headlands, where you will feel close enough to reach out and touch the *Golden Gate Bridge.* (To reach Battery Spencer, take the first exit on the northern side of the *Golden Gate Bridge* and follow the signs to the Marin Headlands, part of the *Golden Gate National Recreation Area.* Battery Spencer is the first turnout as you drive up the hill.) Looking east, through the bridge cables, the city's waterfront curves gently south. Early evening on a clear day is one of the best times to take this photo, when the bridge glows golden and the buildings across the bay reflect the warm light of the setting sun. With a wide-angle lens both the northern and southern anchorages can be included. Don't be perturbed by drifts of fog: At Battery Spencer the fog may float below eye level.

Directions

Introduction

San Francisco is a city of views. No matter which way you turn, there's another splendid sight. Huffing and puffing up the hills, you stop for a moment to catch your breath, and a 360° turn will likely reveal glimpses of an incredibly blue Pacific, a cable car lumbering over the crest of a hill, a lush garden, a stand of towering redwoods, the rooftops of elegant mansions, and skyscrapers, standing in defiance of the next big earthquake, which, experts say, might reduce it all to rubble.

There are many ways to see San Francisco. Standing at the top of Telegraph Hill or *Alta Plaza Park,* the bay sparkles to the north and hills rise from the south. From the *Marina Green* the *Golden Gate Bridge* seems to disappear into the Marin Headlands and Pacific Heights towers to the rear. On a clear day walk over the *Golden Gate Bridge* (it's not golden at all, but a shade of orange called "international") to appreciate the mosaic of homes and other buildings that dot San Francisco's more than 40 hills. Catch a ferry at the *Ferry Building* and survey the city from new perspectives, or careen around its precipitous corners and over its hills, clutching a pole on the running board of a cable car.

Driving a car here can be a hair-raising experience: Waiting on an almost vertical incline for a red light to turn green is not everyone's cup of tea; neither is the momentary thrill of going over the crest of a steep hill into thin air.

Exploring San Francisco on foot is perhaps the most satisfying way to become acquainted with the city's colorful past and exciting present. Compared to a lot of other places, San Francisco's history is quite short: The Ohlone Indians greeted the Spanish soldiers and missionaries in 1776; the Mexicans took control of Spanish-ruled lands when they declared independence in 1821. In 1846 US soldiers marched ashore from the ship *Portsmouth* and raised the American flag. But it was the discovery of gold at Sutter's Mill in 1848 that would forever change the complexion of San Francisco and the West. People came to California for gold; they stayed to build businesses, railroads, and financial empires. And they've never stopped coming.

Most of San Francisco is new—almost nothing goes back more than 150 years, and most is not even 100 years old. Yet each of these seven walks takes you into areas rich in history and stories of the "characters" who made that history. Photographic exhibits along the way on most of the walks provide graphic depictions of what once was here, how it disappeared, and what replaced it. San Francisco's symbol is the phoenix, a fabulous bird from ancient Egyptian mythology that is consumed by fire every 500 years and rises again from its own ashes. More than once San Francisco, too, has been reborn from the ashes—stronger and more beautiful each time.

Walking in San Francisco requires good sneakers or sturdy shoes—you don't feel the hills until you stop at night and your calves begin to ache. You can thank Jasper O'Farrell for the steep streets that comprise the eastern half of the city. In 1847 O'Farrell was hired to plot out the city streets. On paper his very precise grid pattern seemed to work quite well; he failed, however, to take the hills into account. In fact, San Francisco named a street for Jasper O'Farrell—a nice, flat street.

Weather and seasons don't seem to be connected here—unsuspecting summer visitors wear shorts, T-shirts, and sundresses, while San Franciscans wisely wear pants and woolly sweaters. No matter what time of year, a sweater or jacket is a necessity. The residents dress in layers: to be warm in the morning fog, to be more comfortable if the afternoon sun burns away the haze, and to be warm again when the fog rolls in through the Golden Gate. Mark Twain once said, "The coldest winter I ever spent was a summer in San Francisco."

San Francisco is a city to be experienced with all five senses. Vision is only the most obvious—remember to turn around frequently. While climbing California Street to Nob Hill or walking along the waterfront from *Ghirardelli Square* to *Fort Mason,* sometimes the most striking views are right behind you. Sound is everywhere—the unfamiliar, whining sound of a *nan hu,* a Chinese instrument being played on a street corner in Chinatown; strains of *Aida* escaping from open doors and windows in North Beach; and the songs of birds in the gardens bordering the Filbert Street steps. The city is full of wonderful aromas—the *Fragrance Garden* at *Golden Gate Park*'s *Strybing Arboretum;* the musty smell of herbs in Chinatown; and the pungent scents of pastry and garlic in North Beach. San Francisco boasts more restaurants per capita than any other major city. Ethnic restaurants are everywhere; every neighborhood has its cafés and pastry shops. Dim sum can be enjoyed at a tea house on Pacific Avenue, cannelloni at a trattoria on Grant Avenue. And there is the feel of San Francisco—the gentle breezes and the gusts of wind in the financial district and along the shore; the damp morning fog that sometimes blankets the city; and the bright, warm sunshine that burns through to illuminate a very magical place.

Walk 1:
The Financial District

This walk begins at Portsmouth Square, San Francisco's original plaza and the center of activity in the city's early days. Today it is part of Chinatown, but remnants of the early city are close at hand. The best time to take this walk is weekdays during business hours, when the area is alive with people and buildings are open.

Skyscrapers along cavernous Montgomery Street house corporate offices; California Street dazzles the eye as light reflects off the pale stone façades of the West Coast temples of finance—insurance companies and banks do business along this broad street.

No matter what the weather, remember to bring a heavy sweater or jacket: The tall buildings of the financial district block out the warming rays of the sun and the wind sweeps between the towers, adding to the chill. Standing in Portsmouth Square, looking down the gentle slope toward Kearny Street, San Francisco Bay is not visible, but someone standing on this square in 1847 would have been able to see ships at anchor; Montgomery Street was the original shoreline. The town was known as Yerba Buena, which means "good herb," named for the wild mint found growing on the hills. This western outpost of the nation was sparsely populated; Yerba Buena had fewer than 500 residents in 1847.

And then everything changed. One cold morning in January 1848, James Marshall was felling timber for John Sutter at his lumber mill in the Sierra foothills. Something caught his eye, and when he bent down to inspect it, he found it was a nugget of gold. Although Sutter and Marshall tried to keep their discovery secret, word eventually reached Yerba Buena. On this square, in May 1848, a local newspaper editor heralded the news of the discovery of gold along the American River—and the Gold Rush began. Word spread across the country like wildfire, stirring the dreams of many: Lawyers and doctors came, writers came, gentlemen educated at Harvard and Yale came, and within a year more than a thousand men made their way to San Francisco. (Most left their families behind; only 200 or 300 women traveled west during the Gold Rush, and not many children came either.)

Not everyone found what he was looking for in those hills, and by 1851 those who lost heart began to gravitate back to Yerba Buena. By 1855 the city's population had grown to 50,000.

From the north side of the square, cross Kearny Street and walk along Washington Street to Montgomery Street and the Transamerica Pyramid. Covered with cobblestones and wooden planks, Montgomery was considered the first "paved" street in San Francisco. The site of the pyramid was

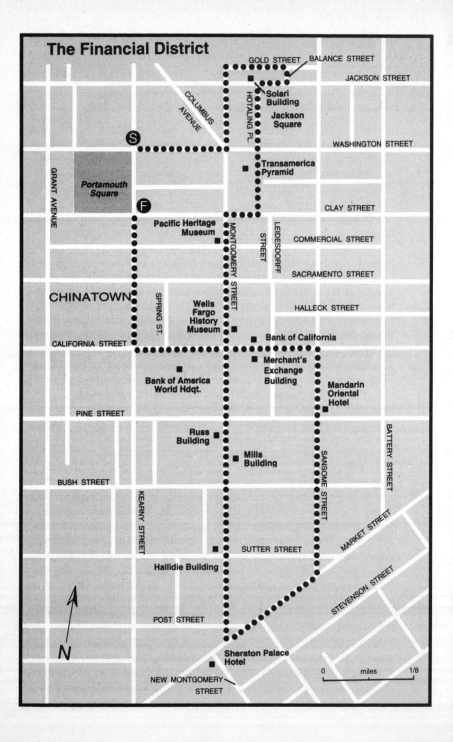

The Financial District

GOLD STREET BALANCE STREET

JACKSON STREET

HOTALING PL.

Solari
Building

Jackson
Square

WASHINGTON STREET

COLUMBUS AVENUE

S

Transamerica
Pyramid

Portsmouth
Square

GRANT AVENUE

F

CLAY STREET

Pacific Heritage
Museum

MONTGOMERY STREET

STREET

LEIDESDORFF

COMMERCIAL STREET

SACRAMENTO STREET

CHINATOWN

SPRING ST.

Wells
Fargo
History
Museum

HALLECK STREET

Bank of California

CALIFORNIA STREET

Merchant's
Exchange
Building

Bank of America
World Hdqt.

Mandarin
Oriental
Hotel

PINE STREET

BATTERY STREET

Russ
Building

Mills
Building

KEARNY STREET

SANSOME STREET

BUSH STREET

MARKET STREET

SUTTER STREET

STEVENSON STREET

Hallidie Building

POST STREET

N

Sheraton Palace
Hotel

NEW MONTGOMERY
STREET

0   miles   1/8

originally the Montgomery Block, an office building, rooming house, and saloon built on piles over the mud. Mark Twain wrote gold country stories when he was a guest here, and legend has it that in the steambaths in the basement he met a fireman named Tom Sawyer—a name he tucked away for a later story. Robert Louis Stevenson and Bret Harte were also among the many literati who lived here at one time or another.

Rising 853 feet into the sky, the Transamerica Pyramid is one of the city's tallest—and most distinctive—buildings; like *Coit Tower,* the *Ferry Building,* and the *Golden Gate Bridge,* it has become a symbol of San Francisco. Built in 1972, it is the headquarters of the Transamerica Corporation, which was set up as a holding company in 1928 by A. P. Giannini, founder of the Bank of America. Ride the elevator to the 27th floor, where the observation room (weekdays only; no admission charge) offers lofty views of the *Golden Gate Bridge,* Alcatraz Island, and *Coit Tower* (phone: 415-983-4000).

Before the pyramid was constructed, Transamerica headquarters were located in the flatiron building across the street, at the junction of Columbus Avenue and Montgomery and Washington Streets. Note the circular entrance and intricate ironwork gate. This building was originally constructed in 1909 as a bank, which it still is: the Chinatown branch of Sanwa Bank California.

Continue walking along Montgomery Street, away from the Transamerica Pyramid. Known as Jackson Square (although there is no square), these Gold Rush–era buildings are some of the oldest commercial structures in San Francisco. The red-brick Belli Building (722 Montgomery), built in 1851, once housed the offices of the "king of torts," attorney Melvin Belli, known to fly the skull and crossbones from the flagpole when he lost a case. Freemasons held their first meeting in California inside the three-story building next door (728 Montgomery). Both buildings survived the 1906 earthquake and fire but suffered severe structural damage in the 1989 temblor.

In 1853 William Tecumseh Sherman presided over the Bank of Lucas, Turner and Company, headquartered in the brick building on the next corner (498 Jackson St.). Sherman's time at the bank was brief; the St. Louis–based institution was discontinued in 1857. Known as a great leader and organizer in San Francisco, Sherman went on to become a famous Civil War general. A few steps beyond is *William Stout Books* (804 Montgomery), crammed from floor to ceiling with books (what else?) on houses, architecture, gardens, design, and more. Gold Street intersects with Montgomery in the middle of the block. The *US Assay Office,* which was at 56 Gold Street, tested the purity of the gold brought in from the fields by melting and pouring it into molds to be stamped and bagged. *BIX* (56 Gold St.; phone: 415-433-6300) serves lunch and dinner, but is best known for its martinis.

Midway down Gold Street a small alley cuts through to Jackson Street. Yerba Buena Cove originally washed over this area, but by 1849 it was clogged with sailing vessels—many of them abandoned when captains and crews jumped ship to head for the gold fields. To accommodate the regular arrival of ships and people, the city began expanding its waterfront to make way for piers, warehouses, and shops; they simply filled in the cove and built right over the abandoned hulls. (Balance Street is named for the ship buried below.)

Antiques shops and offices occupy buildings along Jackson Street that once served other purposes. The one at 415-431 Jackson was the first San Francisco manufacturing site for Ghirardelli chocolates, in 1855. (After leaving his Italian homeland, Domingo Ghirardelli first settled in Peru, where a friend wrote to him that his chocolates would bring delight to the miners in San Francisco.) In 1893 Ghirardelli moved his operations north to the Pioneer Woolen Mill (today known as *Ghirardelli Square*). Anson Hotaling built iron-front Italianate buildings (451-455 and 463 Jackson) as warehouses for his liquor business in the 1860s. The well-built structures survived the 1906 disaster, leading to the following rhyme: "If as they say God spanked the town for being over frisky, why did He burn the churches down and save Hotaling's whiskey?" On the other side of the street (472 Jackson) is the Solari Building; built in 1852, it was once the *French Consulate.* The Jackson Square antiques shops are among the finest in the city, with English, French, and American period furnishings and accessories.

Cross the street and stroll down Hotaling Place, which runs between the two former warehouses. A bas-relief of the Roman goddess Ceres, embedded in the stone wall at 27 Hotaling, marks the entry to what was the workshop of sculptor Ralph Stackpole (1885–1973). The frieze was recovered from the grounds of the 1915 *Panama-Pacific International Exposition.*

A public park across Washington Street, to the left of the Transamerica Pyramid, is home to a grove of redwoods, which grow to be the tallest trees in the world. Benches here afford a good rest spot; it's a humbling, awe-inspiring, yet strangely calming experience sitting beneath these towering trees. A gate at the other end of the park opens onto Clay Street. Turn right to return to Montgomery Street, then turn left and continue to the intersection of Commercial Street.

On the right, the *Pacific Heritage Museum* (608 Commercial; phone: 415-399-1124) occupies the site of the original *US Mint* branch, used to store the substantial quantities of gold and silver that flowed into the city during the Gold Rush era. In 1875 a new building was erected to house the *US Subtreasury.* Note how the Bank of Canton, which operates the museum, has integrated the freestanding structure into its world headquarters design. Changing exhibits inside highlight the artistic, cultural, and economic history of the Pacific Rim. On the lower level the original brick vault and the narrow guard's walk around it can be viewed. The museum is open Mondays through Fridays; no admission charge.

Retrace your steps to Montgomery Street and continue south to 420 Montgomery, where a restored 1867 Concord stagecoach and a collection of gold specimens in their many forms are on display at the *Wells Fargo History Museum.* Open Mondays through Fridays; no admission charge (phone: 415-396-2619). Henry Wells and William Fargo founded the American Express Company in 1850 and Wells, Fargo & Company in 1852. Wells also founded Wells College in Aurora, New York; Fargo was Mayor of Buffalo, New York; and Fargo, North Dakota, is named for him. These two businessmen were an integral part of the Gold Rush and post–Gold Rush eras; Wells Fargo agents posted throughout the West handled a large portion of the 2,300 tons of pure gold that were extracted from the hills between 1848 and 1900. With a fixed price of $20.67 a troy ounce, agents made about a 2% profit on gold. In 1861 the company took over operation of the Pony Express, delivering mail from St. Joseph, Missouri, to San Francisco in just 10 days, at a cost of $2 per half ounce. Only orphans were hired to ride the rugged, 2,000-mile trail. During the late 1860s Wells Fargo ran the stagecoaches across the West. Twentieth-century travelers can sit in a replica of a Pony Express stagecoach on the mezzanine of the museum to get the feel of what it must have been like to ride in this vehicle; with its wooden wheels and suspension system made of leather straps, it was described by Mark Twain as "a cradle on wheels."

California Street crosses Montgomery at the next corner, and double-fronted cable cars run from Drumm and Market Streets past historic bank buildings to the top of Nob Hill, descending on the other side to Van Ness Avenue. Turn left on California to the Merchant's Exchange Building (465 California); built in 1903 it was reconstructed after the 1906 earthquake. An arched skylight extends the length of the lobby, leading to the grand Grain Exchange Hall, the center of commerce around the turn of the century. Ship owners, merchants, and everyone else involved with goods coming and going over the sea lanes gathered under the historic maritime murals painted by William A. Coulter. In 1910 citizens met here to raise funds for the 1915 *Panama-Pacific International Exposition,* collecting $4 million in less than three hours. The murals inside the First Interstate Bank branch office can be viewed Mondays through Fridays.

Another temple of finance, the Bank of California, is located across the street (400 California). William Chapman Ralston, who came to San Francisco as a steamship captain, founded the bank, which opened for business in 1864. Ralston made his fortune in the silver mines—and he lost it there as well. A regular swimmer in San Francisco Bay, he drowned in 1875, shortly after learning that his bank was severely overextended. The current bank building was constructed in 1908.

Though many of the early buildings on this street have come and gone, the sense of history remains. The large walrus heads carved of Sierra granite outside 350 California are all that remain of the Alaska Commercial Building, which stood on this corner from 1908 to 1975. A longtime San Francisco favorite, the *Tadich Grill* seafood restaurant, is a block farther on (240 California St.; phone: 415-391-1849). The fish is always fresh and well prepared. (Try this spot for a late lunch, since the line of business-people outside the door can get quite long, and reservations are not accepted.)

Continue south on Sansome Street, past the entrance to the *Mandarin Oriental* hotel (222 Sansome). Looking nothing like a hotel at all—the first 37 floors of this skyscraper house offices—this well-appointed hostelry is quite elegant and one of the most expensive in the city. From the corner of Sansome and Bush Streets look left to see one of the city's narrowest skyscrapers at 130 Bush. Eleven stories high, this building is only 20 feet wide. Inside the marble courtyard of the Citicorp Center (1 Sansome), flags fly from every nation that has a consulate in San Francisco; grand columns, all that remain of a 1910 bank building, frame the entry to the center. At the far end of the courtyard is a bronze replica of the *Star Girl,* originally created by A. Stirling Calder as the theme piece for the 1915 *Panama-Pacific International Exposition.*

Continue past Sutter Street across to Market Street; walk to the right, past the *Chevron Garden Plaza Park,* winner of the 1990 Strybing Urban Landscape Award, to New Montgomery Street and the entrance to the landmark *Sheraton Palace* hotel. When it first opened in 1875, it was the largest and most luxurious hotel in the world. William Ralston, founder of the Bank of California, and his partner, William Sharon, built the property at a then-staggering cost of $5 million, and because building materials for such a large project were scarce, Ralston built a brick factory in Oakland to supply the building materials. Not one to stint on details, Ralston also purchased a forest to supply the oak flooring and paneling and a factory to make the furniture. On the morning of the 1906 earthquake, famed tenor Enrico Caruso, a hotel guest, ran from the building dressed only in a towel, swearing never to return to San Francisco. Although the hotel survived the quake, it was gutted by the fires that followed. Happily, it was rebuilt and restored to its former glory, opening again in 1909. Reopened several years ago after a $150-million renovation, the *Sheraton Palace* gained, among other things, a conference center and a health spa.

Bathed in golden light filtering through a dome of iridescent glass, the hotel's spacious (110-by 85-foot) *Garden Court* is a delightful place to have afternoon tea; Sunday brunch here is a San Francisco tradition. Before the 1909 reconstruction this area served as the carriage entrance. Other famous guests here have included Thomas Edison, Amelia Earhart, Charles Lindbergh, as well as 10 American presidents, among them Woodrow Wilson and Franklin D. Roosevelt (President Warren G. Harding died in the Presidential Suite in 1923), and such British luminaries as Prince Philip and Winston Churchill.

Cross Market Street and walk north on Montgomery. At Sutter Street, walk a few steps to the left to see the Hallidie Building (130-150 Sutter) in the middle of the block. Designed by Willis Polk in 1917, this is one of the world's most innovative modern buildings, built with a curtain-glass wall.

A Romanesque arch marks the entry to the Mills Building (220 Montgomery). Built by D. O. Mills, the marble entry is rich with decorative detail at the ceiling and along the curved stairways leading to the mezzanine. The 31-story Russ Building (235 Montgomery), constructed in 1928, was the tallest skyscraper on the San Francisco skyline for 40 years. Its vaulted lobby ceiling is intricately patterned; colored chalk emphasizes the mosaic-like details carved into the stone; and detail work continues even to the elevator doors at the back of the entry area.

On the corner of Montgomery and California, dominating the city skyline with its height and its deeply colored carnelian granite, is the 52-story Bank of America World Headquarters (555 California St.). A. P. Giannini founded this institution at the start of the century as the Bank of Italy, to serve the Italian-American community. After the 1906 earthquake he set up a makeshift desk at the edge of the ruins to cash checks and make loans to those who were already planning to rebuild the city. The bank flourished, and in 1930 it was renamed the Bank of America. (A pictorial history of Giannini and the bank and an exhibit of early banking equipment are displayed in an adjacent branch.) A good place to end a walking tour is the *Carnelian Room* (open evenings and for Sunday brunch; phone: 415-433-7500) on the 52nd floor of the bank tower; the restaurant (not great) and cocktail lounge offer panoramic views of the city.

Turn left on California Street. Locals claim the 12 blank-faced statues that line the cornice on No. 580 represent the mayor and the board of supervisors. To return to Portsmouth Square, turn right onto Kearny and walk three blocks.

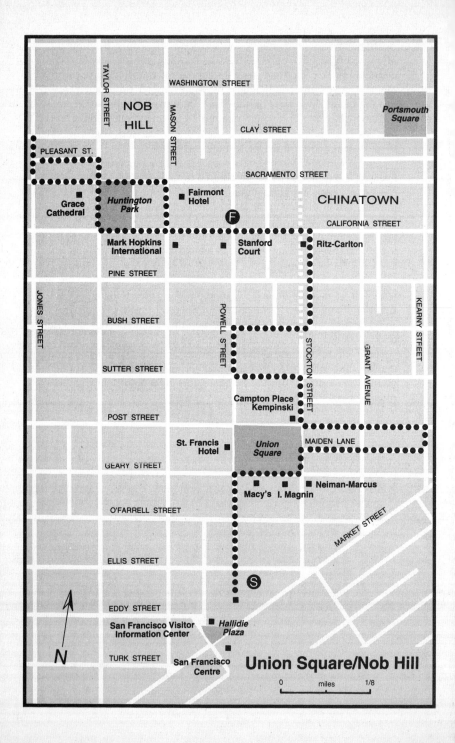

WASHINGTON STREET

TAYLOR STREET

NOB HILL

MASON STREET

CLAY STREET

Portsmouth Square

PLEASANT ST.

SACRAMENTO STREET

■ Grace Cathedral

Huntington Park

■ Fairmont Hotel

F

CHINATOWN

CALIFORNIA STREET

Mark Hopkins International ■

■

Stanford Court

■ Ritz-Carlton

PINE STREET

JONES STREET

BUSH STREET

POWELL STREET

KEARNY STREET

SUTTER STREET

Campton Place Kempinski

STOCKTON STREET

GRANT AVENUE

POST STREET

St. Francis Hotel ■

Union Square

MAIDEN LANE

GEARY STREET

S

■ Neiman-Marcus

Macy's ■ ■ I. Magnin

O'FARRELL STREET

MARKET STREET

ELLIS STREET

EDDY STREET

San Francisco Visitor Information Center

■ *Hallidie Plaza*

TURK STREET

San Francisco Centre

Union Square/Nob Hill

N

0   miles   1/8

Walk 2:
Union Square/ Nob Hill

Before the Gold Rush, San Francisco was a small outpost on the far side of the continent; during the Gold Rush, the City by the Bay grew by leaps and bounds to accommodate miners on their way to the hills and those on their way back. More than $100 million in gold came out of the Mother Lode in the span of four short years, and after the Gold Rush, many new millionaires called San Francisco home. They made their marks on the city, and their legacy remains.

Begin looking for it on Union Square, San Francisco's most famous shopping district. This walk can be completed in just a few hours, unless you're a serious shopper; in that case, several *days* may be required. Start at the cable car turntable at *Hallidie Plaza,* at the intersection of Market and Powell Streets. From this point cable cars travel on two lines up and over Nob Hill and through several neighborhoods before reaching their northern terminuses at either *Aquatic Park* or *Fisherman's Wharf. Hallidie Plaza* is named in honor of Andrew Hallidie, who unveiled the city's first cable car in 1873. The *San Francisco Convention and Visitors' Bureau* offers maps and brochures at the *Visitor Information Center* on the lower level. On weekends and summer afternoons the wait to board a cable car can be 40 minutes or more, but what with the jazzy rhythms of steel drums, the street preachers, the pretzel vendors, and the people watching, time passes quickly.

Look for the flower cart at this corner and at other spots around Union Square. Fresh flowers are sold here every day except Sunday, thanks to Bank of America founder A. P. Giannini. In 1918 Giannini told a flower seller he would like a fresh carnation for his buttonhole each day. Wishing to accommodate this powerful citizen, the vendor tried to get the city's okay for an outdoor flower stand, but he was refused the permit. Word got back to Giannini, who spoke to friends in high places; the vendor got his permit, and Giannini got his fresh carnations.

Just across Market Street is *San Francisco Centre,* a grand glass and brass emporium where the only freestanding spiral escalators in the United States carry shoppers from level to level of chic shops, and up to *Nordstrom,* one of the city's finest department stores. Thread your way through the serious shoppers, souvenir hunters, and panhandlers along Powell to Geary Street and Union Square. This is the heart of San Francisco's shopping district; it also serves as a hub for hotels and entertainment.

Union Square is named for the pre–Civil War demonstrations that took place here in support of the Northern states. Through the years it has been the site of public protests and happenings, as well as a stage for fashion shows and street mimes. Sidewalks lined with benches cut diagonally through the park, which occupies a full square city block. In the center the *Dewey Monument* commemorates Admiral Dewey's 1898 victory over the Spanish navy at Manila Bay during the Spanish-American War. Erected in 1903 the 90-foot granite column and statue withstood the earthquake of 1906.

The *Westin St. Francis* hotel towers over the Powell Street side of Union Square. Flags flown over the front entry signal the nationality of important guests staying at this venerable institution, which was built in 1904. Just inside the front door is the elegant *Compass Rose,* where traditional afternoon tea is served. It was here, over lunch in 1943, that Ernest Hemingway convinced Ingrid Bergman to star in the film version of his novel *For Whom the Bell Tolls.* Across the lobby the Viennese Magneta clock is what San Franciscans refer to when they say, "Meet me under the clock." Legend has it that, no matter what time of day or night, when you stand under the clock, you're sure to see someone you know.

Walk along the Geary Street side of the square, past two of the city's major department stores, *Macy's* and *I. Magnin,* to *Neiman Marcus,* the harlequin-patterned building on the corner of Geary and Stockton Streets. Step through the doors and you are bathed in the amber light of the softly colored stained glass sailing ship on the ceiling of the rotunda, which was installed when the former *City of Paris* department store was rebuilt after the 1906 earthquake. The sailing ship and its inscription, "Fluctuat Nec Mergitur" (It Floats, But Does Not Sink), were the store's emblem. Several generations of boys and girls made annual holiday season visits to the four-story rotunda, to see what was the city's finest, most beautifully decorated *Christmas* tree.

On the Stockton Street side of Union Square is the *TIX* kiosk (see *Music* in THE CITY). On the other side of the street are the *Gucci* and *Hermès* shops.

Maiden Lane, a two-block-long pedestrian mall, starts in the middle of the Stockton Street side of the square. In the Barbary Coast days this passageway of chic shops and galleries was a red-light district. The only Frank Lloyd Wright building in San Francisco is at No. 140. A small, two-level structure built in 1949, it has a gently curved ramp leading from its first floor to the second that is a forerunner of Wright's design for the *Guggenheim Museum* in New York (today it houses an art gallery, open to the public). *Ralph Davies* (77 Maiden Lane) proffers only the most current designer fashions for men and women. Other doors lead into such establishments as *Chanel* and *Robinson's,* an exclusive pet shop.

Emerging from Maiden Lane onto Kearny Street, you're on the edge of the financial district and in the heart of the gallery district. Walk a block south to Geary Street, and you are surrounded by galleries representing contemporary artists—but you have to know where to look, because none of these galleries is located at street level. The *Haines Gallery* (49 Geary,

Fifth Floor) and *Stephen Wirtz Gallery* (Third Floor) show contemporary paintings and sculpture; the *Fraenkel Gallery* (Fourth Floor) houses one of the city's most important photography exhibits. Other galleries are clustered in buildings along Geary and Sutter Streets and Grant Avenue. *Gallery Guide,* a free listing of current shows at galleries and art museums in the city, is available at most galleries. Follow Kearny north to Post Street and turn left again. A flower stand marks the entry to *Gump's* (250 Post St.), where intricately carved jade artwork and fine Oriental furniture are displayed on the third floor, above two levels of crystal, china, and choice housewares.

At the next corner turn right onto Stockton Street. Amid the huge hotels around Union Square, the *Campton Place Kempinski* (340 Stockton) is small, very elegant, very understated, and very expensive. Just off the lobby the *Campton Place* restaurant features first-rate American regional fare at breakfast, lunch, and dinner; Petrossian caviars and champagne or vodka are offered in the bar (see *Eating Out* in THE CITY).

Walk to the left on Sutter Street, stepping in at number 450 to see how the Art Deco façade is continued on the ceiling and elevator doors. The next street is Powell, where the cable cars clang and clatter up to Nob Hill. Instead of attacking the hill head on, climb to the top by zigging to the right at Bush Street and zagging to the left at Stockton. *Masa's* (648 Bush St) is one of the city's finest restaurants (see *Eating Out* in THE CITY); if you decide to dine here, plan ahead, as reservations are definitely required and difficult to get. The alley next door is named for mystery writer Dashiell Hammett, who wrote some of his most famous novels—including *The Maltese Falcon* and *Red Harvest*—while living in San Francisco from 1921 to 1929. A few steps farther down Bush Street, a plaque notes that another author, Robert Louis Stevenson, lived at No. 608 for part of 1879 and 1880.

The white neoclassical structure at the top of the Stockton Street hill was originally designed in 1906 as the Pacific Coast headquarters of the Metropolitan Life Insurance Company, and later housed a college. In 1991 it was renovated and reopened as the *Ritz-Carlton* hotel. On a sunny day views of the financial district skyline from *The Terrace Restaurant* on the second floor make an outstanding backdrop to lunch or dinner, featuring such "California" dishes as grilled *ahi* tuna on rye bread with Moroccan pepper relish, pistachio nuts, and cilantro; grilled veal chops with scallions, shiitake mushrooms, and tarragon-veal essence; and pan-fried loin of lamb with three-pepper compote, lemon–black olive *gremolata,* and seared polenta (600 Stockton; phone: 415-296-7465).

California Street ascends Nob Hill on the other side of the hotel. In the other direction, the street plummets through the financial district to Market Street; the San Francisco–Oakland Bay Bridge looms in the background. Halfway up the block is *Twin's Armoire* (860 California), a closet-size boutique brimming with soft silk frocks and high-fashion hats designed by Rozzalynd and Josephine Wiebe. *Resting Hermes,* a sculpture from the

Italian exhibit of the 1915 *Panama-Pacific International Exposition,* sits in a fenced garden next door at the back of the prestigious, members-only *University Club.*

All three cable car lines cross at only one point—on Nob Hill, at the intersection of California and Powell Streets. The summit, 338 feet above sea level, is one block west. Nob Hill, sometimes snidely referred to as "Snob Hill," took its name from the word "knob," which means a rounded hill or mountain. The derogatory reference evolved from the arrogant extravagances of the "Big Four," *Central* (later *Southern*) *Pacific Railroad* magnates Leland Stanford, Charles Crocker, Mark Hopkins, and Collis P. Huntington.

Before the advent of Hallidie's cable cars, this sandy knob was known as Fern Hill, and city dwellers climbed the sharp incline by foot to picnic and enjoy the view. Only a few modest homes dotted the hill, which was too steep for horse traffic and carts. The cable car made even the steepest slopes traversable, and the Big Four—along with Comstock silver kings James Flood and James G. Fair—began buying up lots at the top of the hill.

The *Stouffer–Stanford Court* hotel (905 California) stands on the corner where Leland Stanford's mansion once stood. Stanford bought all the properties on the south side of the California Street block between Powell and Mason and then sold the higher half of the hill to Mark Hopkins. Trained in the legal profession, Stanford came to California in 1852 and joined his brothers in the grocery business in Sacramento. In 1861 Stanford, Crocker, Hopkins, and Huntington launched the *Central Pacific Railroad,* and in 1862 Stanford was elected Governor of California. By the time the *Central Pacific* and *Union Pacific Railroads* were linked at Promontory Point, Utah, in the spring of 1869, these four cronies were very wealthy men. Stanford's mansion burned in the fires that followed the 1906 earthquake, and the apartment building constructed here in 1911 was later renovated and became the *Stanford Court* hotel. (Also bearing his name is *Stanford University* in Palo Alto, California, which is located on the grounds of his country home and horse-breeding ranch. The school was founded in 1885 in memory of his only child, Leland Stanford Jr., who died at age 15.)

On the crest of the hill, Mark Hopkins built his grand palace at a cost of $3 million—a lot of money for a man who got his start selling hardware to miners during the Gold Rush. Like the other redwood mansions on Nob Hill, it burned in the 1906 fires. The *Mark Hopkins* hotel (1 Nob Hill) was built as a residential hotel on the same corner in 1926, and was later renovated to accommodate travelers, eventually joining the Inter-Continental chain. Cocktails at the *Top of the Mark* (phone: 415-392-3434) are worth the lofty price for the 360° view.

One mansion still stands at the top of Nob Hill—the brownstone building sitting staunchly in the middle at 1000 California Street. Redwood was the building material of choice in those days; it afforded the flexibility for the ornate architecture these wealthy men admired. In 1855 only James Flood, who began his days in San Francisco as a saloon keeper and made his millions through the Comstock silver mines, chose dark, heavy stone. He also installed a bronze fence (at a cost of $30,000) around the perimeter of the property and reportedly hired one full-time employee just to polish it. The Flood mansion is now the headquarters of San Francisco's very exclusive *Pacific Union Club.*

The *Big Four* restaurant in the *Huntington* hotel (1075 California St.; phone: 415-771-1140) could almost be a museum devoted to these railroad men; its dark-paneled walls are hung with posters, photographs, and other fine memorabilia from the railroad and silver barons.

Grace Cathedral, one of the largest church buildings in the West, is on the opposite corner, facing Taylor Street. Begun in the 1920s, this concrete Gothic edifice was finally consecrated in 1964. Its sweeping front staircase was completed in 1994, but other renovations will continue on through this year. The bronze doors at the entrance are replicas of Ghiberti's *Doors of Paradise* at the Baptistry in Florence. Stained glass windows inside depict such outstanding contemporary citizens as astronaut John Glenn, social worker Jane Addams, and poet Robert Frost. Murals depict the history of the church and the city.

Land for *Grace Cathedral* was donated to the Episcopal church by the Crocker family after the 1906 earthquake and fire. In the 1870s Charles Crocker bought up the lots on the block surrounded by California, Taylor, Sacramento, and Jones Streets. Only one man, Nicholas Yung, held out and refused to sell his parcel. To spite him, Crocker built a 30-foot-high wall around three sides of the man's house.

Benches in *Huntington Park,* across the street from the cathedral, provide a place to rest and look around. David Colton, who as vice president of the *Southern Pacific Railroad* was sometimes referred to as a member of the Big Four and a Half, built his mansion on this spot. Collis Huntington's widow purchased it from Colton's widow, and in 1915 the land was donated to the city.

There were very few happy tales to come out of these baronial residences, and those that burned down were not immediately rebuilt. Yet despite the imposing presence of hotels, Nob Hill is still a residential neighborhood. Walk west on Sacramento Street and turn right onto Jones, continuing to its intersection with Clay for another perspective of the Transamerica Pyramid. Then retrace your steps to the middle of the block and walk left down Pleasant Street. Before turning right on Taylor to return to the top of the hill, cross the street to the cozy little *Nob Hill Café* (1152 Taylor; phone: 415-776-6500). Pasta dishes dominate the menu; fresh juice and coffee also are served.

Continuing along Sacramento Street behind the *Pacific Union Club,* walkers approach the Italian Renaissance–style *Fairmont* hotel (950 Mason). The tall building on the corner of Sacramento and Mason is the Brocklebank

Apartments (1000 Mason St.), designed by Weeks and Day, the architects of the *Mark Hopkins* hotel. Kim Novak called this elegant high-rise home in Alfred Hitchcock's haunting 1958 film *Vertigo.* The *Fairmont,* built by the daughter of silver king James G. Fair, was almost complete when the ground shook early on the morning of April 18, 1906. Fires raged for three days, and when it was all over, only the Flood mansion and the shell of the *Fairmont* were still standing on Nob Hill. The grand hotel was quickly rebuilt, reopening exactly one year after the earthquake. The lobby harkens to another era. Red patterned carpets and red upholstery, marble pillars, dark wood paneling, and gold-leaf moldings combine to give a sense of the opulent lifestyle that once flourished on Nob Hill. Beyond the lobby the hallway leading to the main ballroom is hung with an outstanding collection of photographs showing the city before and after the earthquake. At the rear of the hotel a glass elevator runs up the outside of the building, carrying passengers to the *Crown Room,* where lunch and dinner buffets are served daily (phone: 415-772-5000). The experience of the "outdoor" elevator ride and the view from the top are memorable.

To complete the walk, follow California Street back to Powell, and take the cable car back to the Market Street turntable.

Walk 3: North Beach

Washington Square's broad green expanse comes as a surprise in the middle of a crowded, bustling neighborhood. This much loved, much used park has been here since the 1850s, when it was one of the few green spaces easily accessible to city residents. San Francisco's first rodeo took place here in the 1850s. In the aftermath of the 1906 earthquake and fires, a tent city sprang up here to shelter some of the thousands who were left homeless. Today young families spread blankets on the grass to soak up the sunshine, old men park themselves on the benches facing Union Street, and most mornings there are pockets of people practicing t'ai chi.

The name North Beach is a relic of the city's earliest days, before the waterfront was filled in, when Yerba Buena Cove was the natural harbor and Portsmouth Square was the city's main plaza. In those days the area was indeed the north beach.

Two statues grace the park's lawn. Benjamin Franklin stands in the center of the square at the top of an old fountain (no longer spouting) donated by Gold Rush dentist H. D. Cogswell. Although the fonts are labeled Congress, Vichy, and Cal Seltzer, the fountain spewed out only plain tap water. The second statue, erected with funds donated to the city by Lillie Hitchcock Coit, commemorates the men who served in San Francisco's volunteer fire departments from 1849 to 1866.

Twin spires rise to the heavens from the Romanesque *Church of Saints Peter and Paul* on the Filbert Street side of the park. Construction was started in 1924 and took nearly 15 years to complete; Cecil B. De Mille filmed scenes of *The Ten Commandments* on the site. Inside stained glass windows and mosaics line the way to the altar and a replica of Michelangelo's Vatican *Pietà*. Joe DiMaggio grew up in this neighborhood and was married—not to Marilyn Monroe—in this church. Two old-style celebrations begin here each year: the blessing of the fishing fleet each fall and the *Columbus Day Parade.*

Although the population of North Beach is no longer predominantly Italian, the cafés, restaurants, and old family businesses remain. When first settled, North Beach was briefly considered a fashionable residential area. As those stylish citizens moved to newer areas, this became the Latin Quarter, home to Chilean, Mexican, Peruvian, Portuguese, Spanish, French, and Italian immigrants who journeyed to California to join the Gold Rush. Starting in the 1890s with an influx of Italian fishermen and laborers, the Latin Quarter evolved into Little Italy. Over the next decades the Italian population grew, and as the people became more prosperous, they began migrating from North Beach. By the 1950s a more bohemian subculture began to occupy the area.

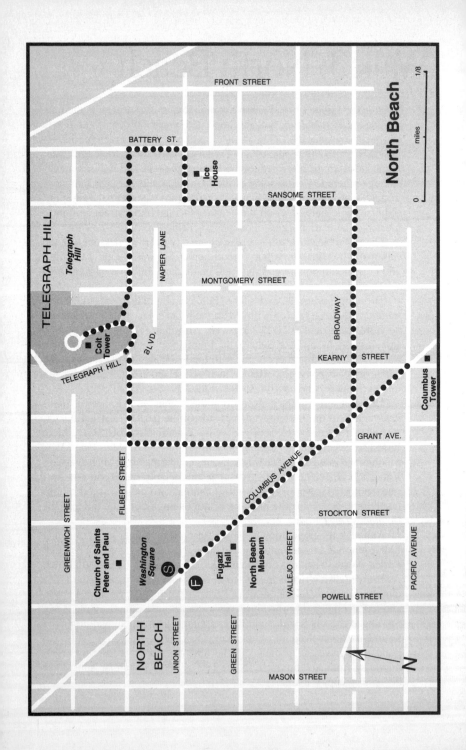

North Beach

FRONT STREET

BATTERY ST.

Ice
House

SANSOME STREET

TELEGRAPH HILL

Telegraph
Hill

NAPIER LANE

MONTGOMERY STREET

Coit
Tower

BROADWAY

TELEGRAPH HILL

KEARNY   STREET

Columbus
Tower

BLVD.

GRANT AVE.

COLUMBUS AVENUE

FILBERT STREET

STOCKTON STREET

GREENWICH STREET

Church of Saints
Peter and Paul

Washington
Square

Fugazi
Hall

North Beach
Museum

VALLEJO STREET

PACIFIC AVENUE

POWELL STREET

NORTH
BEACH

UNION STREET

GREEN STREET

MASON STREET

N

0   miles   1/8

Walk south along Columbus Avenue and experience the pulse of North Beach. Cafés, bakeries, and restaurants line the broad, crowded avenue. *Mario's Bohemian Cigar Store* (566 Columbus) is a good place to soak in the excitement over a *caffè latte.* A short side trip across Green Street leads to the *Club Fugazi* (678 Green St.; phone: 415-421-4222), where *Beach Blanket Babylon*—a zany cabaret-style musical with outrageous costumes and massive headdresses that light up—has developed a loyal following over the past 18 years (see *San Francisco's Sounds of Music* in DIVERSIONS). Built in 1912, this landmark building was once a community meeting hall for the Italian community. Artifacts and old photographs at the *North Beach Museum* (1435 Stockton St., at the corner of Columbus, on the mezzanine of the Eureka Bank; phone: 415-391-6210) offer insights into the neighborhood's past. Open Mondays through Fridays; no admission charge.

Good smells seem to come from almost every door along Columbus Avenue. The *Caffè Roma Coffee Roasting Co.* (526 Columbus) displays its equipment in the front window, and the strong aroma of freshly roasted beans fills the street—stop in for beans to take home or a cup of coffee to go. Just beyond the ancient street clock, sweet smells lead to *Stella Pastries* (446 Columbus), where patrons pick and choose from among the cookies, cakes, and panettone baked fresh here each day. *Caffè Roma* (414 Columbus; phone: 415-391-8584) serves breakfast and lunch (try the pizza with homemade sauce), and people watchers can sip coffee and watch the constant parade of passersby. At the *Molinari Delicatessen* (373 Columbus) shelves are stocked from floor to ceiling with peppers, olive oils, pasta, cheese, and other good things to eat. For a lingering experience visit the *Stinking Rose* (325 Columbus). From *bagna calda* (whole garlic cloves in olive oil) to garlic ice cream to bottles of vintage garlic wine, it's a shrine to the pungent bulb.

The *City Lights* bookstore, the literary center of North Beach, is at 261 Columbus just across Broadway (phone 415-362-8193). Opened by poet Lawrence Ferlinghetti in 1953, it was the country's first all-paperback bookstore. It was Ferlinghetti who published Allen Ginsberg's notorious poem *Howl,* as well as the works of poets Gary Snyder, Gregory Corso, and others. San Francisco columnist Herb Caen coined the term "beatnik" from Jack Kerouac's description of himself and these other writers as "the Beat Generation." Next door is the *Vesuvio Café* (255 Columbus; phone: 415-362-3370), another focal point of the Beat era. The alleyway between the bar and bookstore has been renamed for Kerouac. Across from the bookstore at 242 Columbus, the *Tosca Café* (phone: 415-391-1244) is a favorite late-night spot among opera buffs; the Wurlitzer jukebox plays opera only, and the most popular drink is made with hot chocolate and brandy.

Columbus Tower stands at the foot of Columbus Avenue. This flatiron building completed just after the 1906 earthquake has copper-clad windows now weathered to a soft green. In the 1960s the building was owned by the *Kingston Trio;* in the 1970s Francis Ford Coppola bought and restored this landmark, now used for office space.

Backtrack up Columbus Avenue, across Broadway, to continue up Grant Avenue. Storefronts on this street display fine clothing and postcards next to Chinese laundries and hair salons. Behind some of the covered windows are Chinese sewing shops. Many of the Italian shops along this street have been run by the same families for 70 or 80 years. *Caffè Trieste* (at the corner of Grant and Vallejo St.; phone: 415-392-6739) is not one of those old-time family operations, but it is something of a San Francisco tradition. On Saturday afternoons, beginning at 1 PM, the sound of Italian opera spills out of the jammed café. Francis Ford Coppola reportedly wrote and rewrote the script of *The Godfather* here.

Farther up Grant Avenue there are remnants of the old Italian neighborhood on both sides of the street. Step into *Figoni Hardware* (1351 Grant), the oldest such store in San Francisco (established in 1907); it's like stepping back in time. Nothing much has changed in this family-run business; stock stretches from ceiling to floor. At 1358 Grant the *Panama Canal Ravioli & Tagliarini Factory* operates from a storefront.

Looking up and down the streets of North Beach, the houses seem to fill every available inch of space: Front steps spill right out onto the sidewalk; houses are side by side by side. *Washington Square* is the only spot of green. Or is it? Walk up Green Street to No. 478, where a trellised walkway threads through the shade of trees and ferns, past the entrance to a restaurant and into a sunny, open patio bordered by flowers and aging fig trees. Small garden spaces are tucked away behind some of the houses. The building at the back of this garden was originally an indoor bocce court.

Return to Grant Avenue and continue north. The *Shlock Shop* (1418 Grant) is a dark, cramped hole-in-the-wall with shelves of hats lining the walls and more hats dangling from the low wooden ceiling. Porkpies, bomber helmets, fedoras—they're all here. Its owner, artist Avrum Rubenstein, also owns *The Scene,* the art gallery that has been next door since 1953. If the gallery is closed, peek at the paintings through the window. In every picture the subject is wearing a hat!

At 1434 Grant the late-night *Savoy-Tivoli* (phone: 415-362-7023) opens onto the street for outdoor drinking and dining. The *R. Iacopi & Co. Meat Market* has been making sausages at the corner of Grant and Union Street since 1910 (pick up a sandwich for a picnic at *Washington Square* or *Coit Tower*). On the opposite corner the aroma of freshly baked bread escapes through the door of the *Italian French Bakery.*

At the next corner turn right and begin the trek up Filbert Street to *Coit Tower,* at the top of Telegraph Hill. This section is as strenuous as it looks. To reach the tower with less exertion, walk one block back to Stockton and Union Streets and take the No. 39 Coit Tower bus to the top of the hill. In 1850 a watchman was posted at the top of this hill. At first sight of a ship entering the bay, a semaphore signal was sent to San Francisco's merchants and citizens waiting for news and mail from the rest of the world. In 1853 the first telegraph station in California was built here.

As you continue your climb, remember to turn around and look out over the city for a breathtaking view of Russian Hill. It's also a good excuse to stop and catch your breath on this precipitous incline. At the corner of Filbert and Kearny look south for views of the Transamerica Pyramid and the Bank of America building. From here continue the climb via the Filbert Street steps to Telegraph Hill Boulevard. On the right, at 115 Filbert, is one of the few remaining shacks used to shelter those who were left homeless by the 1906 earthquake and fires. A few steps farther, a break in the trees frames a view of the Bay Bridge, Treasure Island, and the East Bay hills. Treasure Island was the site of the *1939–1940 Golden Gate International Exposition,* and is now the property of the US Navy.

Once you reach the summit of Telegraph Hill, the view on a clear day is 360°. Sailboats, tankers, and ferries traverse the bay; naval vessels and ocean liners are frequent visitors. Alcatraz—the onetime federal maximum-security prison known as "The Rock"—sits empty in the center of the bay. Beyond Alcatraz is *Angel Island State Park,* used as an immigration center for Asian immigrants during the first half of this century and as a detention camp during World War II. It's accessible by ferry from San Francisco via the *Red & White Fleet* (phone: 415-546-2805), departing from Piers 41 and 43½. Bring a bicycle or a picnic—Angel Island offers nothing more than great views, a dozen miles of paths, and solitude. To the west the *Golden Gate Bridge* reaches across the mouth of the bay into the Marin Headlands. The highest point on the opposite shore is Mount Tamalpais. Coin-operated telescopes are strategically placed around the Telegraph Hill parking lot for close-up views.

Coit Tower is open daily; the admission charge includes access to the restored murals and the elevator ride to the top.

Enjoy the panoramic view (this is a perfect place to capture the city on film; see *A Shutterbug's San Francisco* in DIVERSIONS), then walk back to the Filbert Street sign and turn left. (Or, return to *Washington Square* by taking the No. 39 Coit Tower bus, which leaves the parking lot approximately every 20 minutes.) On the east side of Telegraph Hill, Filbert Street is a staircase leading past the gates of houses hidden on the hillside. At the bottom of this first section of steps is Montgomery Street. Crossing Montgomery, the staircase continues next to 1360 Montgomery. This Art Deco building, with its etched-glass entrance, ocean-liner motif, and silver-painted nautical murals, was home to Lauren Bacall in the 1947 movie *Dark Passage,* which also starred Humphrey Bogart.

Ancient wooden plank steps wind past a jungle of wonderful gardens dedicated to Grace Marchant, who devoted more than 30 years of her life to creating these verdant spaces on the site of a former dump. Birds sing loudly from their perches along this hillside; roses and fuchsia bloom profusely during late spring and summer. Some of the houses along this stretch of Filbert Street, like the cottages at Nos. 228 and 224, date back to the 1870s. The building at 222 Filbert was once a grocery store. (See "Climbing Filbert Steps" in *Quintessential San Francisco,* DIVERSIONS.) At Napier Lane the dense vegetation gives way to a sloping garden of flowers and ferns. Paved with planks, this relic of the Gold Rush era cuts to the left but goes nowhere. Near the bottom of the hill wooden steps give way to a short, steep segment of concrete. To the right the bare, rocky hillside testifies to the years of quarrying that scraped away this side of Telegraph Hill for construction of retaining walls and fill for the bay as the shape of the waterfront was stretched and changed.

Between Telegraph Hill and the waterfront are the brick expanse of Levi Plaza and the many refurbished brick warehouses that have survived the city's growth. Levi Strauss & Co. has San Francisco roots dating back to 1853, but the famous blue jeans came later. In 1871 a saddlebag maker named Jacob Davis from Reno, Nevada, used copper rivets to reinforce the seams of work pants made from denim purchased from Levi Strauss. The next year Davis and Strauss applied for a patent on this method of securing pockets and other stress points, and soon the pants were de rigueur among longshoremen and loggers alike.

Just across Sansome Street benches throughout the plaza beckon weary walkers, and water splashes soothingly in a granite fountain in the center. Beyond it is *Il Fornaio* (1265 Battery St.; phone: 415-986-0100), a popular place to stop for a meal, a snack, a glass of wine, or a cappuccino. Or take out treats for a picnic on the lawn on the other side of Battery Street. The *Fog City Diner* (1300 Battery St.; phone: 415-982-2000) is across the street; there's always something interesting—such as red curry mussel stew or garlic custard with sherry-cayenne mayonnaise—on its regularly changing menu. A good time to stop in is between 2 and 4 PM; it's less crowded, and you can linger over a second—or third—cup of coffee (see *Eating Out* in THE CITY).

Turn right on Battery and walk past the old warehouses, turning right again on Union Street. The Ice House (151 Union) was built about 1915 to store the huge blocks of ice brought from Alaska for use throughout the city. Later ice was made here. After several incarnations, the brick buildings are now used as office space.

Continue left on Sansome Street to reach Broadway, which in the city's early days was the main route into town from the passenger docks. Walking right on Broadway brings you to a mélange of restaurants, strip joints, jazz clubs, punk and heavy-metal music clubs, and tattoo parlors. Upstairs at 506 Montgomery Street, above the barkers and hubbub of the street, *Finocchio's* (phone: 415-982-9388) offers topnotch nightclub acts by female impersonators. No matter which way you look, the action never seems to stop on this stretch of turf.

To return to *Washington Square,* turn right on Columbus Avenue.

Walk 4: Chinatown

A tour of Chinatown is a must for people who like to indulge their curiosity. You could take a quick walk down one of its main thoroughfares and say you had seen Chinatown, but the real Chinatown is a maze of streets and alleys, with distinctive sounds and unfamiliar scents. Chinatown spills out of shopfronts onto the sidewalks—exotic vegetable stands and tacky souvenir kiosks reach out to passersby; shop doors open and the warm, doughy smell of dim sum is added to the general aroma. But there is still another Chinatown hidden behind many of its closed doors. This walk is for the explorer.

Begin at Portsmouth Square, one of the only open places in this compact and densely populated section of the city. From morning until night the park's bright red benches are occupied by Chinese men talking and gaming. Grandmothers and mothers look after young children in the playground on the lower tier of the square.

During the 19th century most of the Chinese immigrants came from Guandong Province in south China, leaving their homeland because of floods and drought, and because of the Taiping Rebellion between 1850 and 1864. San Francisco's Chinese population was about 450 in 1850, but when word of the Gold Rush reached China, many more Chinese came here to the "Gold Mountain," hoping to find riches. By 1852 the Chinese population in California had reached 20,000.

Follow Kearny Street to Commercial Street, where the *Chinese Historical Society of America*'s museum (650 Commercial; phone: 415-391-1188) uses photographs, maps, and artifacts to trace the history of the Chinese people in San Francisco. Start the walk here to get a better sense of the neighborhood as you crisscross through the streets and alleys. Open Tuesdays through Saturdays from noon to 4 PM; no admission charge. (This walk ends close to Commercial Street, in case the museum is closed when you begin.)

Return to Portsmouth Square by walking along Kearny to Washington Street and turn left. The Bank of Canton's red and green pagoda (743 Washington) was once the Chinese Telephone Exchange, where operators were required to memorize the numbers of everyone living in Chinatown. At the corner, turn right on Grant Avenue, one of Chinatown's main arteries. It's usually crowded on this street, where out-of-towners mingle with local residents doing their daily shopping and errands.

To Western eyes it may seem a jumble at first, but behind the flimsy souvenirs are hidden treasures. Chinese paintbrushes and bottles of ink are sold at *Chew Chong Tai & Co.* (905 Grant). Brushwork paintings are displayed at the back of the little shop, where they also can be framed for you. *Ten Ren Tea & Ginseng Co.* (949 Grant) imports the finest teas from China, selling as many as five different grades of highly prized teas such as oolong

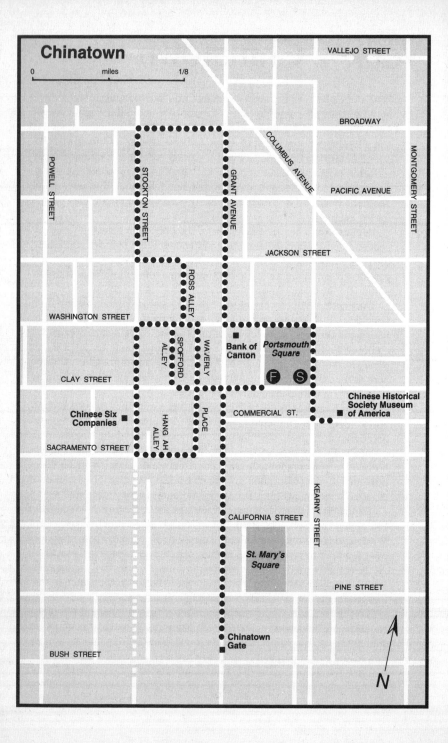

Chinatown

0 — miles — 1/8

VALLEJO STREET

BROADWAY

COLUMBUS AVENUE

POWELL STREET

STOCKTON STREET

GRANT AVENUE

PACIFIC AVENUE

MONTGOMERY STREET

JACKSON STREET

ROSS ALLEY

WASHINGTON STREET

SPOFFORD ALLEY

WAVERLY PLACE

Bank of Canton

Portsmouth Square

CLAY STREET

HANG AH ALLEY

F S

Chinese Historical Society Museum of America

Chinese Six Companies

COMMERCIAL ST.

SACRAMENTO STREET

CALIFORNIA STREET

KEARNY STREET

St. Mary's Square

PINE STREET

Chinatown Gate

BUSH STREET

N

and jasmine. Stop and chat with one of the staff here; each is a veritable encyclopedia on tea. On a recent visit we learned that the best tea comes from the youngest leaves and is handled with the most care; it is also the most aromatic. Sometimes an old Chinese man sits along the street here playing a *nan hu*—a two-stringed violin-like instrument played with a bow. Bazaars and hardware shops display cookware next to paper kites, mahjongg sets, and ceramic ornaments.

Grant Avenue is a colorful place, but a closer look at the buildings reveals that they are not Chinese in design. These brick and concrete structures were built by non-Chinese landowners after the 1906 earthquake and subsequent fires leveled the original Chinatown. Brightly painted pagoda roofs, balconies bearing Chinese characters, and other design elements were added later. Lampposts with giant lizards holding up each lantern were created specifically for Grant Avenue.

Food shops line this street north of Pacific Avenue. Produce vendors sell Chinese mustard greens, bok choy, snow peas, and long beans as well as winter melon, mangoes, oranges, and finger-length bananas. Row after row of whole fish rest on mountains of ice in the fishstores. Pressed smoked duck and Chinese bacon hang in the windows of the meat markets; *Kwong Jow Sausage* (1157-1161 Grant) sells Chinese sausage. Poultry is purchased live in Chinatown at shops like *Ming Kee Game Birds* (1122 Grant). More general markets sell noodles, sauces, and canned and dried goods. There are incongruities here, too, such as loaves of sliced white bread stacked alongside exotic vegetables, and tanks of small aquarium fish sold in the same shop that sells fish for food.

During the 1850s and 1860s much of the food sold in these shops was grown by Chinese men returning from the gold fields. Many began farming on land beyond the city limits, selling their produce in Chinatown and elsewhere in the city. Others left town and moved to shrimp-fishing villages in what is now Marin County. From 1865 to 1869 Chinese laborers made up 90% of the work force completing the western section of the transcontinental railroad.

Walk left one block on Broadway, turning left again onto Stockton Street. This thoroughfare has fewer tourists than Grant, but the crowds are even denser. There are many restaurant choices in the area: *Yuet Lee* (1300 Stockton at Broadway; phone: 415-982-6020) specializes in seafood—clams in black bean sauce is one of their most popular dishes; if you're here (and hungry) late, it's open until 3 AM. Dim sum is a popular lunch or snack choice in Chinatown. Good places in Chinatown to try it are *New Asia* (772 Pacific Ave.; phone: 415-391-6666) and *Pearl City* (641 Jackson St.; phone: 415-398-8383). Once you're seated, watch for the waitresses pushing steam carts or carrying trays and point to whatever looks good. Servings are small, so you can sample as many things as you like. *Siu mai* (pork dumplings), *ha gow* (shrimp bonnets), and steamed or baked pork buns are standard selections. At the end of the meal, the server counts the number of plates to determine your bill.

Turn left off Stockton onto Jackson Street and follow it half a block to Ross Alley. The warm, sweet scent of cookies baking wafts through the door of the *French Adult Fortune Cookies* shop (56 Ross Alley). Each cookie is baked flat in an individual griddle; as it emerges from the oven, a woman picks it up and folds it into shape, placing the paper fortune within. Beyond the bakery, incense from the *Sam Bo Trading Co.* (14 Ross Alley) fills the air. Statues, red candles and banners, and papers burned in religious ceremonies are sold here. Occasionally, other doors open and close, allowing fleeting glimpses into Chinatown's many sewing shops. At the end of the alley, turn right onto Washington Street to return to Stockton Street, and then turn left.

There are churches and temples throughout the neighborhood. On the corner of Stockton and Washington Streets, a red pagoda tops the *Chinese United Methodist Church.* Farther down Stockton, at Clay Street, the *Kong Chow Temple* is located above the *US Post Office,* on the fourth floor.

Lions stand guard at the entrance to the Chinese Six Companies headquarters next door (843 Stockton). On a somewhat gray street, the brightly painted building with pagoda roofs stands out. The *Chinese Consolidated Benevolent Association,* as it is also known, was established in 1854 to unify and control the businesses of the many family associations in Chinatown and their dealings with non-Chinese. Cross to the opposite side of Stockton Street to see the entire building, with its traditional green tile roof and Chinese red doors.

At Sacramento Street turn left, past Hang Ah Alley, site of the *Hang Ah Tea Room* (phone: 415-982-5686), one of Chinatown's oldest dim sum restaurants, to the *First Chinese Baptist Church* and the start of Waverly Place. This two-block section of Chinatown houses many of the family benevolent associations. When Chinese men emigrated to California, the women and families stayed behind. There were only about a thousand Chinese women here in 1880, so *gongso* (family associations) were formed as affiliations of people with the same surname, to provide a kind of substitute family. Today these associations provide recreation and social services. There are two more temples on Waverly Place, the *Norras Temple* (109 Waverly) and the *Tin How Temple* (125 Waverly). Their brightly painted upper levels are best viewed from the other side of the street. Although they are in use throughout the day, these houses of worship are open to the public.

At the end of Waverly, turn left onto Washington and then left again onto Spofford Alley. Once a central thoroughfare in Chinatown, it often seems almost deserted, except for a constant clacking noise and the sound of excited voices from the mah-jongg games going on behind closed doors and shaded windows. But this alley has seen much activity. The bright red brick front at No. 36 Spofford is the *Chee Kung Tong* (Chinese Freemason) building, where Sun Yat Sen and other revolutionaries met to plan the overthrow of the Manchu government. Many confrontations between tongs, rival secret fraternal societies organized for gambling and vice, took place in this alley, too, until the *General Peace Association* was founded in 1913 in an attempt to calm the open violence. At the end of the alley, walk left along Clay to Grant Avenue, and continue to the right.

In the early days of Chinatown, Grant Avenue was known as Dupont Street. San Franciscans and other Californians were blatantly prejudiced against the Chinese, whose clannishness, customs, and religions were so different from their own. In 1855 the city's supervisors estimated that 30,000 Chinese people lived in a 12-block area. Space was crowded; 20 or more men slept on narrow shelves stacked up along all four sides of a room in which one person might have felt cramped. A Cubic Air Act was passed in 1870, requiring 500 cubic feet of space for each person sleeping in a room. The law was enforced only in Chinatown.

Immigration continued at a steady pace, approximately 10,000 a year. By 1876 prejudice was rampant, and both candidates in that year's presidential campaign took strong anti-Chinese positions. The federal government enacted the Chinese Exclusion Act in 1882, which prohibited entry to Chinese laborers; it was repealed in 1943.

The earthy smell of herbs is persistent throughout the streets of Chinatown. Ginseng, piled high in herb shop windows, traditionally comes from Changpai Mountain in China and is considered very valuable. Royal jelly, a secretion from worker bees believed to promote long life and energy, is sold in several forms. A well-stocked herb shop can have more than 3,000 different medicinal items, such as pieces of spotted deer antler, deer tail extract, and pearl powder, in the drawers and jars that line the walls. Based on the symptoms described, the herbalist selects the healing ingredients and pounds them into a fine powder to be made into a soup or tea. Bark from various trees, gums, nuts, and flowers are also used. (Li Po-Tai, a well-known Chinatown doctor in the mid-1800s, treated many non-Chinese patients, including Governor Leland Stanford and railroad man Mark Hopkins.)

Immersed in this Asian culture, California Street and the cable car bells come as a shock. *Old St. Mary's* is on the corner of California and Grant; constructed in 1854 of red brick hauled around Cape Horn and stone that was quarried and cut in China, this was the first cathedral erected in California. The Chinatown Gate, built in 1970, is another two blocks down Grant Avenue. Intricately carved ivory, fine cloisonné, and jade carvings are displayed in windows along the way.

Retrace your steps on Grant Avenue, turning right on Sacramento Street. Chinese children study calligraphy, language, history, and literature behind the iron gates of the *Nam Kue School* (755 Sacramento St.).

Return to Portsmouth Square by going back to Grant Avenue and turning right and right again onto Clay Street. To complete a tour of Chinatown, cross the pedestrian bridge from the square to the *Chinese Cultural Center* (750 Kearny St., inside the *Holiday Inn*; phone: 415-986-1822). Open Tuesdays through Saturdays, this is where works by contemporary Chinese artists are exhibited and books about Chinese art and culture are for sale.

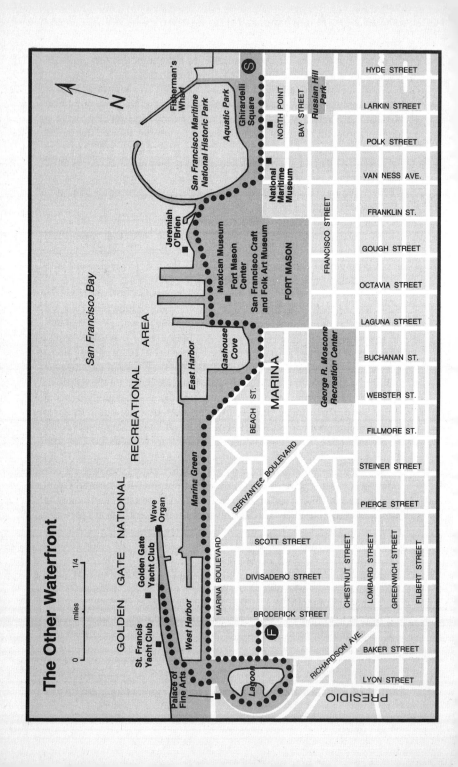

The Other Waterfront

HYDE STREET

LARKIN STREET

POLK STREET

VAN NESS AVE.

FRANKLIN ST.

GOUGH STREET

OCTAVIA STREET

LAGUNA STREET

BUCHANAN ST.

WEBSTER ST.

FILLMORE ST.

STEINER STREET

PIERCE STREET

SCOTT STREET

DIVISADERO STREET

BRODERICK STREET

BAKER STREET

LYON STREET

CHESTNUT STREET

LOMBARD STREET

GREENWICH STREET

FILBERT STREET

Russian Hill Park

NORTH POINT

BAY STREET

FRANCISCO STREET

FORT MASON

George R. Moscone Recreation Center

MARINA

RICHARDSON AVE.

CERVANTES BOULEVARD

MARINA BOULEVARD

BEACH ST.

PRESIDIO

National Maritime Museum

Ghirardelli Square

Aquatic Park

San Francisco Maritime National Historic Park

Fisherman's Wharf

Jeremiah O'Brien

Mexican Museum

Fort Mason Center

San Francisco Craft and Folk Art Museum

Gashouse Cove

East Harbor

Marine Green

RECREATIONAL

AREA

San Francisco Bay

GOLDEN GATE NATIONAL

Wave Organ

Golden Gate Yacht Club

St. Francis Yacht Club

West Harbor

Palace of Fine Arts

Lagoon

0   1/4
miles

Walk 5:
The Other Waterfront

After *Disneyland, Fisherman's Wharf* is the second most visited spot in California. Everyone knows about this picturesque area where harbor seals bark and swim alongside the docked fishing fleet, and street vendors sell cups filled with Dungeness crab. Arriving by cable car is the most special approach. *Victorian Park* is the terminus of the Powell-Hyde line, which stops at the top of Hyde and Lombard Streets—the up side of what is probably the most crooked street in the world. From here the cable car rushes down to the waterfront, where streets are jammed with visitors going in and out of souvenir shops and galleries. The *Fisherman's Wharf* of postcard fame is to the right. *The Cannery* (2801 Leavenworth St.; phone: 415-771-3112), a brick complex of shops and restaurants tucked into a former fruit-canning building, houses the *Museum of the City of San Francisco* (phone: 415-928-0289). Open Wednesdays through Sundays; no admission charge (see *Museums* in THE CITY). Street performers juggle knives and flaming torches, artists sketch quick caricatures, and musicians play their tunes. And only on *Fisherman's Wharf* can you find the amazing human jukebox: Insert a coin into a homemade, man-size, carton-like contraption, request a song, and a trumpet player appears from behind a curtain and plays for you. Jefferson Street stretches past fishing boats and postcard stands, past steaming cauldrons filled with crab, all the way to *Pier 39* (see *Special Places* in THE CITY).

But there's another waterfront, with spectacular views of the city's hills and the *Golden Gate Bridge,* a place where residents come to sun, fly kites, and generally relax.

Start at the cable car turntable at the bottom of Hyde Street, just a short walk from the wharf. The *Buena Vista* (2765 Hyde St.; phone: 415-474-5044) is famous for Irish coffee, which was invented here. People come here to rub shoulders; it's crowded and noisy, and everyone shares tables. Street vendors peddle jewelry and sweatshirts along the stretch of Beach Street leading to *Ghirardelli Square,* an outstanding example of how historic buildings can be recycled for new uses. This San Francisco landmark, at the corner of Beach and Larkin Streets, with its familiar neon sign, was built as the Pioneer Woolen Mill in 1864 when the area was far beyond the city's boundaries. When Domingo Ghirardelli outgrew his manufacturing facility on Jackson Street in 1893, he moved his chocolate company here and added new structures to accommodate his growing business. After the candy makers moved to the East Bay in 1960, a preservation-minded citizenry passed a law limiting the height of buildings in the area. Happily, many of the older buildings that otherwise would have been demolished were saved, making *Ghirardelli Square* the country's first shopping complex in a restored historic industrial building. Today the many levels house shops, restaurants, plus the *Ghirardelli Chocolate Manufactory* (phone: 415-474-3938). Warm, chocolaty aromas bring you right to the door of this candy store and ice cream parlor; you can see how chocolate is made daily at the back of the shop while indulging in a sinfully sweet ice-cream sundae.

Everything is ship-shape across the street at the *National Maritime Museum* (*Aquatic Park;* phone: 415-556-3002), which chronicles the history of shipping, beginning with the Gold Rush era. Heroic figureheads, sections of masts, and nautical artifacts recovered from wrecks are on display beside finely detailed model ships. Open daily; no admission charge. Beyond the museum the path goes past a *bocce* court and down toward the water.

From here it's just a short climb to that other waterfront. A paved roadway curves gently up the hill on the other side of the municipal pier. The sound is different here; water hits against the rocks below, and the breeze rattles and shakes the trees. Stop at the top of the hill and look behind: The northern edge of the city rises and falls along the many hillsides. Look ahead: The *Marina Green* reaches to the west, leading the eye to the towering dome of the *Palace of Fine Arts.* In the background the *Golden Gate Bridge* connects San Francisco with the hills of Marin County

Joseph B. Strauss wasn't the first person to imagine a bridge across the mile of water at the Golden Gate, but it took his unique blend of skills as an engineer, romantic poet, and fine public speaker to pull off such a challenging project. Critics scoffed from start to finish. At some points the water at the mouth of the bay is 64 fathoms (384 feet) deep. Combined with the currents and the tremendous flow of water regulated by the tides, debunkers claimed a bridge would cost many times the $27 million Strauss estimated. However, his passion for the project helped convince the voters to approve a bond issue in 1930, and A. P. Giannini, founder of the Bank of America, helped finance the bridge. Construction began in 1933, with men working against the forces of nature, including towering waves and winds up to 70 miles per hour. Ten workers fell to their deaths in a scaffolding accident; in another accident 19 men were saved by a safety net stretched more than a mile from shore to shore. The *Golden Gate Bridge* opened in 1937, on schedule and within budget.

Each cable along the span is three feet in diameter and 1½ miles long, made up of enough strands of wire to circle the earth three times. The towers rise 750 feet above the ocean; the road deck is 220 feet up. From the beginning the famous span has been painted "international orange." It shimmers in the sunset and stands out against the bank of fog that often slips through its towers. Repainting the bridge is an ongoing project; as soon as workers complete the job, they go back to the other end and start all over.

Look down to the pier at *Fort Mason,* below you. The SS *Jeremiah O'Brien,* the only Liberty Ship still in its original state, is moored here. Because cargo ships were in short supply at the beginning of World War II, the principles of mass production were applied to shipbuilding and 2,751 Liberty Ships were constructed. Go aboard daily for a closer look. Admission charge.

People come to picnic and to play in the meadow at the top of the pathway. Steps ease the descent to *Fort Mason Center,* which occupies the covered piers and four warehouses down below. During World War II, 1½ million troops and 23 million tons of cargo were shipped to the Pacific from this port of embarkation. *Fort Mason*'s history actually goes back to 1797, when the Spanish ruled Northern California. They called this area Punta Medanos (Point Sand Dunes), and placed a five-gun battery here to protect the bay from invaders. In 1853 *Fort Mason* became a US military reservation, and during the Civil War 12 cannons were installed. Congress turned it over to the *National Park Service* in 1972, and today it is the hub of the *Golden Gate National Recreation Area.*

Something is always happening along this waterfront: At *Fort Mason Center,* a unique partnership between the *National Park Service* and a nonprofit foundation presented some 15,000 events last year. Space is used for children's programs as well as classes in martial arts, fiction writing, health, recreation, and visual arts; there are also fine arts performances, as well as workshops and exhibitions on the environment and education. Among the more than 500 participating organizations are the *Mexican Museum, San Francisco Craft and Folk Art Museum, Museo ItaloAmerican,* and the *Magic Theatre.* For details call 415-979-3010 (recorded schedule), or stop at the office in Building A for a monthly calendar.

Eating at *Fort Mason* is another pleasurable experience. *Greens* (see *Eating Out* in THE CITY) serves an ever-changing vegetarian menu featuring fresh ingredients grown at the Zen Center farm in Marin County. The black bean chili is particularly warming on cold, foggy days. Fresh baked goods served here are also sold at the *Tassajara* bakery counter at the front of the restaurant. A wall of windows opens out over sailboats at anchor in Gashouse Cove, with a panorama that includes the *Golden Gate Bridge.*

Follow Marina Boulevard west toward the *Golden Gate Bridge.* The *Marina Green,* the grassy stretch along the shoreline, is a favorite open space among city dwellers. The brisk breeze that pushes sailboats over choppy waves makes this a perfect spot for kite flying. Sun worshipers come out to work on their tans when the sun shines—no matter what the temperature. Pay telescopes along the waterfront afford a closer view of Alcatraz and Marin County.

Across the boulevard Spanish Colonial– and Mediterranean-style houses—with their stucco walls and tile roofs—stand side by side. These dwellings, which sell in the $2 million range, are relative newcomers; most were built during the 1920s and 1930s. This is the Marina district, an area familiar to many because of the 1989 earthquake, when pictures of collapsed buildings and fires caused by ruptured gas mains were on the front page of every newspaper in the country. Careful scrutiny will reveal some unpatched cracks and lopsided features, remnants of that shaker. One reason the Marina district was so seriously affected by that earthquake is the composition of the ground beneath these homes—it's almost all fill.

Anticipating the opening of the Panama Canal in 1914, San Francisco petitioned Congress to designate the city as a world's fair site to host the celebration. The Marina district, then a muddy backwater known as Harbor Cove, was selected as the site, and new ground—created by piling topsoil on top of sand dredged from the bottom of the bay—suddenly appeared. After the 1906 earthquake and fires, the 1915 *Panama-Pacific International Exposition* was a showcase to attract travelers and businesspeople from around the world and to show them that San Francisco had recovered quickly and rebuilt itself bigger and better than ever.

No expense was spared in creating this legendary event. In the 1950s it cost approximately $10 million to build *Disneyland;* it cost $50 million to design and construct the 1915 Exposition buildings. There were 11 palaces to house agricultural and industrial displays and exhibitions showing off the latest innovations. Largest and tallest was the *Tower of Jewels,* rising from the center of the exposition. Each night spotlights caught the dazzle of 100,000 individual jewels, each dangling from the tower on its own string, with a mirror behind to reflect the light back into the night. Ford manufactured 18 cars a day in a temporary plant, and a five-acre working model of the Panama Canal took up one corner of the amusement zone. An "Overfair Railway" was constructed to transport visitors over the 635 acres of fairgrounds. In the 10 months it was open, it had nearly 19 million visitors.

Only one building, the *Palace of Fine Arts,* remains (in reproduction) from the 1915 exposition, located on the other side of Marina Boulevard at Baker Street. (The fair's structures were never intended to be permanent, and all the other buildings were demolished soon after it closed in December 1915.) A favorite among San Franciscans, the palace was left standing; used over the decades by the Army and by the city, it began to crumble. In the 1960s Walter S. Johnson, a philanthropist who lived on Baker Street, grew tired of looking at the ruin and began a campaign to finance a reproduction of the original palace. What cost under $1 million to construct in 1915 cost almost $7.5 million to rebuild.

Architect Bernard Maybeck designed the original Roman structure with its fine Greek details. The archway, covering five acres, had 120 galleries to display the art of 43 states and 25 nations. The "Weeping Ladies," each 22 feet tall, cling to boxes at the top of columns along the colonnade. Maybeck planned to have plants and vines growing from those boxes, and the "Weeping Ladies" were supposed to water them, but money ran out before that project could be completed. At the center of the palace, gigantic columns rise to support the rotunda, which reaches 150 feet high. Six panels around the outside of the dome represent Art.

In front is a lagoon formed from an inlet from the bay. The manmade island in the center is a bird sanctuary. Walk around the lagoon to get a sense of the grandeur of this place. In fact, the soft golden glow of the lofty dome at sunset can also be seen from many parts of the city (it's also lighted at night). No wonder newlyweds favor the spot for their wedding pictures.

The *Exploratorium* (3601 Lyon St.; phone: 415-561-0360 for recorded information), a hands-on museum of science, art, and human perception, is located inside the archway. (See *Museums* in THE CITY.)

Just beyond the *Palace of Fine Arts,* across Lyon Street, is the *Presidio of San Francisco.* A former Army base that was turned over to the *Golden Gate National Recreation Area* in 1994 for use as a park, it was one of San Francisco's earliest settlements. Mexico's Spanish rulers established a military outpost there in 1776, when they sent explorers north along the coast of California. After gaining independence from Spain, Mexico took control of the *Presidio* in 1822; in 1846 the United States took over the 1,400-acre complex. From the Civil War era, when Union troops trained here, on, the *Presidio* was used as a training ground. Following the 1906 earthquake and fires, those left homeless were housed in refuge camps here.

Return to the starting point of this walk by taking the No. 30 Stockton bus from the corner of Beach and Broderick Streets to the corner of Hyde Street and North Point, one block from the cable car turntable.

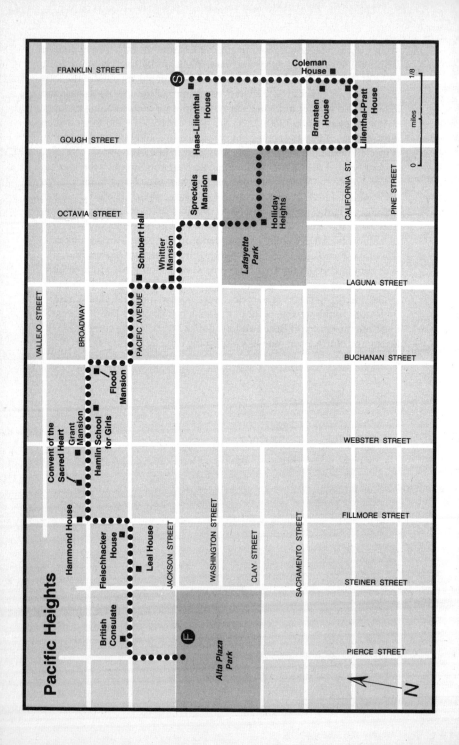

Pacific Heights

FRANKLIN STREET

GOUGH STREET

OCTAVIA STREET

LAGUNA STREET

BUCHANAN STREET

WEBSTER STREET

FILLMORE STREET

STEINER STREET

PIERCE STREET

VALLEJO STREET

BROADWAY

PACIFIC AVENUE

WASHINGTON STREET

JACKSON STREET

CLAY STREET

SACRAMENTO STREET

CALIFORNIA ST.

PINE STREET

Coleman House

Haas-Lilienthal House

Bransten House

Lilienthal-Pratt House

Spreckels Mansion

Holliday Heights

Lafayette Park

Schubert Hall

Whittier Mansion

Convent of the Sacred Heart

Grant Mansion

Flood Mansion

Hamlin School for Girls

Hammond House

Fleischhacker House

Leal House

British Consulate

Alta Plaza Park

N

1/8

miles

0

Walk 6: Pacific Heights

San Francisco's early hub was Yerba Buena Cove. Ships from around the world docked at the wharfs, and immigrants and newcomers built up neighborhoods and businesses nearby. Sand dunes and steep hills stretched to the west, making transportation to these outlying areas difficult.

Pacific Heights was largely devoted to farming. Cows grazed on the hillsides, and dairies operated at the bottom of the hills, in what is now known as Cow Hollow/Union Street.

The invention of the cable car, however, changed things. People began building homes farther and farther west of the downtown hub and traveling by cable car to their businesses each day. Pacific Heights was an ideal place for residential development. Sweeping views from the northern slopes were dazzling, and two large public parks gave a sense of openness to the neighborhood. Upstanding merchants built grand homes, other citizens bought "tract" houses—the Victorian row houses that still dot many quiet streets. Meanwhile, the wealthiest of the wealthy erected palatial mansions using the most costly building materials. Although this route is designed to give you a feel for the neighborhood and its architecture, it comprises mainly private homes; therefore you must be content to gaze at these landmarks from the sidewalks.

The Haas-Lilienthal House (2007 Franklin St., near Jackson St.) is a good place to begin exploring the many beautiful Victorian homes and mansions that still remain. Alice Haas Lilienthal lived in this house from 1886, when it was built, until her death in 1972. The rounded tower, pointed roofs, and geometric shapes along the façade are all characteristic of the Queen Anne style. The garden next door was added toward the turn of the century, after a neighboring house was purchased and demolished. The Haas and Lilienthal families, well-respected merchants, have a long history in San Francisco. The Lilienthals were in the liquor business, in which they joined forces with the Haas family. Haas's descendants today own the Oakland *A's* baseball team and Levi Strauss. Owned and operated by the *Foundation for San Francisco's Architectural Heritage* (phone: 415-441-3000), this home is open for tours on Wednesdays from noon to 4 PM and Sundays from 11 AM to 5 PM. There is an admission charge. (The foundation also offers historic tours of Pacific Heights on Sundays at 12:30 PM.)

The house next door (2003 Franklin) is representative of another Victorian style known as Stick Eastlake, developed in the late 1880s after the work of interior designer Charles Eastlake. Stick Eastlake–style houses emphasized vertical design elements, using square-cornered bay windows, as opposed to the slanted bay windows of the Italianate style.

Continue south along Franklin Street toward California Street, stopping to look at the red brick Bransten House at 1735 Franklin. Families lived in close proximity during this era of San Francisco's history; fathers built houses next door for their married daughters, and brothers and sisters lived within walking distance of one another. William Haas, father of Alice, built this house in 1904 as a wedding present for his eldest daughter, Florine, and her husband, Edward Bransten (Bransten was the "B" in MJB Coffee). Across the expanse of green lawn, unusual for this part of San Francisco, is the Coleman House, built in 1895 for Edward Coleman. Although it is now home to the law firm of Choulos, Choulos & Wyle, the restored Queen Anne building has had a checkered history. At one point it was used as a boardinghouse; the hippies who came next removed some of the French stained glass windows visible across the lawn. By happy coincidence, during the restoration process, the missing glass was found at a flea market.

Turn right on California to the Lilienthal-Pratt House at No. 1818, which was built in 1876 as a wedding present from Louis Sloss to his daughter and her husband, Ernest Lilienthal—who later became Alice Haas's in-laws. Built in the Italianate style, it incorporates the popular slanted bay windows. Wooden detail work gives the impression of stone.

In this more formal era, when people stayed at home to receive callers on certain days of the week, Victorian residences had two sets of front doors. Open outer doors were an invitation for visitors to knock. A servant would disappear with the visitor's calling card and return the card with a bent corner to indicate whether or not the person at home would accept the social call.

Edward Coleman's brother, John, bought the house next door (1834 California), which was built in 1876 for Isaac Wormser of S & W (Sessman & Wormser) Fine Foods. Wormser's was a more simple Victorian, in the Italianate style, but Coleman added the Queen Anne–style turret on the left side of the house and extra rooms under the gabled roof line to help accommodate his 10 children. Front views can be misleading; the 41-room house extends deep into the lot. The tall, evergreen "monkey puzzle" tree in the garden to the right was a familiar sight in Victorian gardens.

At the corner Gough Street leads gently uphill. At Sacramento Street, turn right for a brief side trip to take in a group of standard San Francisco Victorian row houses (Nos. 1911, 1913, 1915, 1919, and 1921). Unlike the Victorians seen so far, these middle class residences were not designed by architects but built from a pattern, using the various standard elements available from the mills. Redwood was the popular building material of the day, favored for its fire-resistant qualities and the ease of pressing intricate designs into the wood for ornamentation. Because lots in this part of town measured only 25 feet across, most row houses were built with false fronts, to extend the height at the roofline. These are landmark buildings, so changes to the exteriors today—including gardens, colors, and façades— are strictly controlled. Restoration and renovation of these fine old structures is big business in the Bay Area; wood mills specialize in matching any

Victorian element, and there is even a wallpaper company that will match any sample.

Return to Gough Street and turn left into *Lafayette Park,* a verdant, nine-acre area spread over four square blocks. During the post–Gold Rush era, squatters occupied much of the land outside of downtown San Francisco. In some cases they were even paid to stay there by real estate developers who hoped to stake a claim to the property. The condominiums at 1925 Gough, in the park, are the legacy of one squatter the city never could evict successfully. He built his house in the park; when he died the property was eventually passed on to others and developed.

Across the street the Victorians at 2000 and 2004 Gough are examples of how quickly styles change. The 1885 Stick Eastlake–style house at No. 2000 shows hints of the Queen Anne style to come. In 1889 the same builder constructed the house next door at No. 2004; note the round corner tower and the elaborate Queen Anne–style woodwork.

Climb the steps to the top of *Lafayette Park* for outstanding views in all directions. This is the highest point in Pacific Heights, and after the 1906 earthquake many San Franciscans climbed this hill to survey the damage in the eastern sector of the city. Van Ness Avenue, two blocks east of the park, became the fire break. Many of the city's most extravagant mansions lined that overly wide avenue, but when the fires that followed the earthquake spread west, officials decided that the only way to protect the rest of the city was to dynamite these palaces to prevent them from fueling the flames.

Samuel Holliday, a successful lawyer and owner of the *Overland Stage Company,* was also a squatter. In 1866 he built Holliday's Heights at the very peak of the hill in Lafayette Park, adding an observatory several years later. During his lifetime the house was a literary gathering place. Holliday successfully fought the city's efforts to evict him, but after he died, officials seized and demolished the house, leaving only the ring of trees that surrounded it.

Many of San Francisco's wealthiest and most influential citizens built their mansions on the slope sliding north from *Lafayette Park.* Descend the Octavia Street steps in the center of the park and then turn right on Washington Street, where you will find the Spreckels Mansion (2080 Washington), which dominates the street. Adolph Spreckels, one of sugar king Claus Spreckels's 13 children, built this "sugar palace" in 1913 using Utah limestone. One of the largest homes in Pacific Heights, it has a six-car garage and a swimming pool enclosed in a separate building at the back of the property. Frank Sinatra fans may recognize the driveway entrance on the right side of the house, because it was used for outdoor shots of the entry to the *Chez Joey* nightclub in the movie *Pal Joey.* Spreckels family members lived here until about 1990, when the mansion was sold to novelist Danielle Steel.

Attitudes toward San Francisco homes changed after World War I, when the wealthy began to favor very large apartments instead of mansions. In the salmon-colored apartment building at 2006 Washington, each floor is a single apartment; some have as many as 24 rooms. The purchase price for a floor is estimated at between $5 million and $6 million.

Senator James D. Phelan built the yellow brick Italian Renaissance Revival mansion (2150 Washington) two blocks beyond the Spreckels Mansion in 1915. The view from the back of the house down to San Francisco Bay and the Marina district is unobstructed, making it a perfect location to entertain the dignitaries from around the world who came to the city in that year for the *Panama-Pacific International Exposition*. After dinner Phelan could dazzle his guests with the nightly fireworks and the sight of the sparkling *Tower of Jewels* in the center of the fairground.

Return to Octavia Street, with its trees and wavy curbs meant to discourage automobiles. The lawn sweeping past the Spreckels Mansion pool enclosure down to Jackson Street is a rare sight in San Francisco. Walk left on Jackson Street to the Whittier Mansion (2090 Jackson) on the next corner. William F. Whittier, one of the founders of the Fuller-O'Brien Paint Company, built this 31-room home of red Arizona sandstone in 1896, taking full advantage of such "modern" amenities as electricity instead of gaslights. The mansion was purchased by the German government for use as a consulate in 1941 and seized by the US government shortly afterward. The *California Historical Society* acquired it for its headquarters in 1956, and tours of the furnished dwelling were offered periodically until it was sold in 1991 to a Hong Kong businessman, for a residence again. Turn right on Laguna Street and continue along to Schubert Hall (2099 Pacific Ave.), on the corner of Laguna and Pacific Avenue. The *California Historical Society* now occupies this mansion, which was built in 1904 for another member of the Spreckels family. The society's *North Baker Library,* devoted to California and western history, is open to the public during limited hours (phone: 415-567-1848).

Follow Pacific Avenue to the left for one block, then walk right on Buchanan to Broadway. To the left is the Flood Mansion (2120 Broadway), where lions guard the entrance to what is now the very exclusive *Hamlin School for Girls*. Silver king James C. Flood built this imposing edifice for his daughter in 1901. Although it appears to be built of stone, the exterior is actually painted wood. The school purchased the mansion in 1928 from the *University of California* regents, who had acquired it in 1924 after Miss Flood took up residence at the *Fairmont* hotel.

Schools also occupy the mansions on the next block, between Webster and Fillmore Streets. The *Convent of the Sacred Heart School* is located in the marble palace in the middle of the block (2222 Broadway). James L. Flood, son of James C., commissioned this home in 1912, to be finished in time for the *Panama-Pacific International Exposition*. The intricate metal grillwork at the front door is quite elegant and unusual. Flood's wife lived here until 1939, when she turned the house over to the Order of the Sacred Heart. The block's brick buildings are also part of the school, connected by bridges at an upper level. *Hammond House* was built in 1905 and later became *Stuart Hall for Boys* (2222 Broadway); the *Grant Mansion,* within the same block, was built in 1897.

On a clear day one of San Francisco's most famous panoramic views can be seen from the corner of Fillmore Street and Broadway. Turn left on Fillmore, remembering to look back over your shoulder. Turn right onto Pacific Avenue.

Full-grown trees hide the fronts of some of the spectacular homes along Pacific Avenue. Others, like the 1905 white-trimmed, red brick Fleischhacker House (2418 Pacific), are protected by iron fences and gates. Across the street (2475 Pacific) is the Leal House, one of the oldest homes in Pacific Heights. Built about 1850 as a ranch house, it was surrounded by 25 acres used for grazing cattle. On the next block the stone and brick building on the double lot at 2516 Pacific is the living quarters of the British consul. The brick portion of the dwelling, on the right, was built in 1880; the stone section, on the left, was added about 1920. In the days after the 1906 earthquake and fires, when 250,000 residents were left without shelter, this house served as a soup kitchen.

Although the 1906 earthquake was responsible for some destruction in the city, the fires that followed caused the most damage. Broken water mains hampered efforts to extinguish the flames, and many of the buildings that withstood the shaking were reduced to ashes. Based on that experience, huge cisterns were installed under streets throughout the city to hold an emergency supply of water in case of future fires. One of these is buried at the intersection of Pierce Street and Pacific.

Alta Plaza Park, the other four-square-block hilltop retreat in Pacific Heights, is at the top of Pierce Street, to the left. From the peak you can see the bay to the north and Twin Peaks to the south. Fillmore Street, two blocks to the east, is a bustling area lined with shops and eateries. Locals flock to *Pauli's Café* (2500 Washington St., at the corner of Fillmore St.; phone: 415-921-5159) for a hearty brunch featuring a wide choice of omelettes served with home fries. For lunch try *Vivande Porta Via* (2125 Fillmore St.; phone: 415-346-4430) for its daily pasta special, or *Leon's Bar-B-Q* (1915 Fillmore St.; phone: 415-922-2436), a popular spot for ribs and hot links. If you're in the mood for exotic fare, go to *Oritalia* (1911 Fillmore St.; phone: 415-346-1333) for Asian favorites, including pork and shrimp dumplings and spicy Indonesian chicken *satay.*

To return to the Haas-Lilienthal House, walk six blocks farther east, or take the No. 83 Pacific Avenue bus (from the corner of Fillmore and Washington) east on Washington to Franklin.

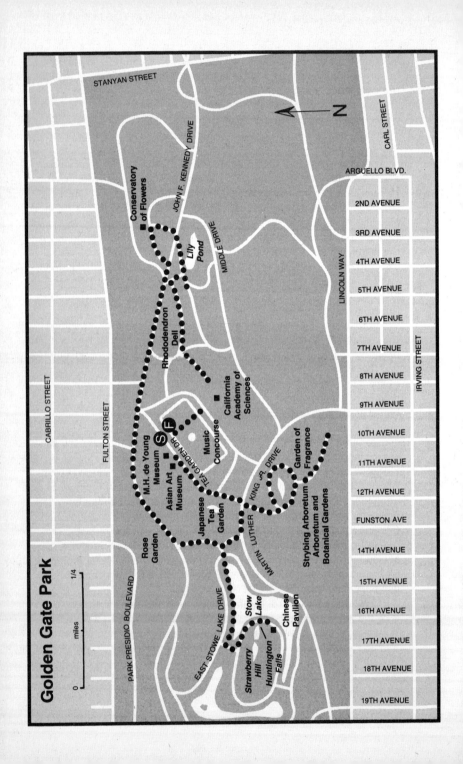

Walk 7: Golden Gate Park

New York City has *Central Park,* Paris has the *Tuileries,* and San Francisco has *Golden Gate Park.* Beginning in the 1870s, anybody and everybody went to Golden Gate Park to see and be seen. Victorian era visitors traveled by carriage to see the gardens and to hear outdoor concerts. The railroad brought more visitors to the gardens and glades; in 1894 they came to see the *California Midwinter International Exposition.* Contemporary visitors come to stroll or jog, to bicycle or roller-skate, to study plants and flowers, to read the Sunday paper, to enjoy the wide open spaces, and to view outstanding collections of art.

Walking through the entire park—3 miles long and a half-mile wide, with paths and roadways winding over hills and through meadows—would take more than a day, but a morning or afternoon spent on this walk will give you a chance to explore the open spaces and the intimate corners in the eastern and central part of the park.

Begin at the *M. H. de Young Memorial Museum,* where Earl Cummings's 1917 sculptures *Indian Boy with Pipe* and *Mountain Lions* rest in the *Pool of Enchantment* at the entrance. Closed Mondays and Tuesdays; admission charge (phone: 415-750-3600; 415-863-3330 for recorded information). See *Museums* in THE CITY. The café inside is one of the few places in the park—aside from the occasional refreshment stand—to sit down for lunch or a snack.

The gates of the *Japanese Tea Garden,* built in cooperation with one of San Francisco's sister cities, Osaka, are to the right as you exit the museum. Temple architect Kensuki Kawata designed the traditional decorative features for these cypress gates, which were constructed without nails, and the unpainted baked-clay roof tiles. Both the tea garden and the original gates are remnants of the Japanese village constructed by Oriental art specialist George Turner Marsh for the 1894 exposition.

When you walk through the gates, you leave behind the traffic and hubbub of the busy concourse and enter a garden of calm and quiet. Japanese gardener Makoto Hagiwara is credited with the original landscape. (Hagiwara also invented fortune cookies, although Chinese merchants later copied the idea and marketed them.) A dwarf tree garden showcases specimens tended and trained by the Hagiwara family, who cultivated the garden from 1895 until 1942, when they were forced to relocate during the war. To protect the trees in their absence, the Hagiwaras entrusted them to a local landscape architect, who later sold them to Dr. Hugh Fraser. At the time of her death, his widow bequeathed the trees to the tea garden, where they are once again on display. The *Japanese Tea Garden* is open daily; admission charge (phone: 415-752-4227). See *Glorious Gardens* in DIVERSIONS.

From the *Japanese Tea Garden* gate on Hagiwara Tea Garden Drive, walk to the right and cross Martin Luther King Jr. Drive to the north entrance of the *Strybing Arboretum and Botanical Gardens.* Free tours are offered daily (phone: 415-661-1316). See *Glorious Gardens* in DIVERSIONS.

Exiting via the north gate, return to the opposite side of Martin Luther King Jr. Drive, go left, and take the paved path through the trees, veering left at the fork and climbing the short flight of steps to reach Stow Lake. While walking through the park, note the large number of coniferous trees; Monterey pine, Monterey cyprus, and blue gum comprise 90% of the trees in *Golden Gate Park.* In 1870, when William Hammond Hall was hired to survey the proposed park in what was known as the Outside Lands, sand dunes covered the 1,017-acre parcel. Any trees that once had grown in the wind-shifted sand had been cut for firewood during the Gold Rush, and the idea of a park in this barren hinterland was widely ridiculed. Frederick Law Olmsted, designer of New York City's *Central Park,* said trees would never grow on the bleak dunes, and one newspaper reported that it was so windy that a blade of grass would need four posts to keep it from blowing away. Hall, the first park superintendent, had faith in the idea of a grand park and believed it could be properly planted. While he was camping one night in the dunes, his horse kicked over a feedbag of barley. Waking after a night of gentle rain, Hall discovered that the barley had sprouted. Using that new information, he first planted barley on the dunes, followed by deep-rooted lupine to hold the sand in place. As the ground became more stable, he began to add trees. Hall's general plan for the park respected the existing contours.

Listen for the sound of water falling over rocks, and look for a green pagoda roof while walking right, along the edge of the manmade lake. Cross the bridge to Strawberry Hill, the island in the center, and walk to the left, in the direction of the waterfall. Scrub oak, California cherry, and wild strawberries once covered this hill; juicy blackberries now grow on bushes along the path in summer. Look for turtles sunning themselves on logs in the lake. (To experience Stow Lake from the water, continue along the path to the boat house instead of crossing the bridge. Rowboats, pedal boats, and battery-powered boats can be rented daily.)

Huntington Falls was built with money donated by railroad magnate Collis P. Huntington; stairs on either side lead to the top. (For serious hikers, dirt paths wind around the hillside to the top of Strawberry Hill, which offers sweeping views of the city.) Flat stepping stones pave the path across the bottom of the falls, and a misty spray dampens the air. The brightly painted Chinese pavilion just around the bend offers a good place to rest in the shade. A gift from the city of Taipei, another of San Francisco's sister cities, it was shipped here in 6,000 pieces. Retrace your steps past the falls, over the bridge, and back to the right, to the point where you crossed the road. At the bottom of the steps, take the path to the left, which skirts the back of the *Japanese Tea Garden* and emerges on John F. Kennedy Drive.

Flowers are in bloom from May through November in the *Rose Garden* across the road. Buttery-yellow New Day, creamy Class Act, reddish-pink Olympiad, and the strongly scented Fragrant Cloud grow in some of the 63 perfectly pruned beds labeled to identify the many varieties of old roses and hybrids. Lawn areas around the roses are a good place to sit and sun; the large grove of redwoods next to the garden offers a shady alternative. Redwoods, with their reddish-brown fibrous bark and evergreen needles, are the world's tallest trees, often reaching well over 200 feet at maturity.

Follow John F. Kennedy Drive to the *Conservatory of Flowers,* the oldest building in *Golden Gate Park.* This Victorian palace of white-painted glass was modeled after *Palm House* in *Kew Gardens,* London, and shipped around Cape Horn in pieces, to be erected on the grounds of James Lick's San Jose mansion. Lick died before the conservatory could be put up, and it was eventually purchased by the city of San Francisco from his estate. Enter at the central dome, where the feel of humid air and scent of warm, wet earth are immediately noticeable. Bananas, palm trees, and flowering vines grow in one section; collections of rare orchids in another; and a changing display of seasonal flowers in the west wing. Open daily; admission charge (no phone). See *Glorious Gardens* in DIVERSIONS.

Leaving the conservatory, the steps between the palm trees lead to a tunnel under John F. Kennedy Drive. Emerging on the other side, continue to the right. At the first fork, follow the dirt and bark path to the left, to the point where a number of paths converge. Several steps along the path to the left is the Lily Pond. Here, in what was once a rock quarry, birds sing, turtles sun themselves, and ferns and forest surround the quiet waters. Thick stands of weeds grow quickly here, so park workers periodically drain and clean the pond. At one cleaning a cache of jewelry, other valuables, and weapons was discovered at the bottom, presumably dumped by thieves on the run.

Backtrack to the intersection of paths and walk straight ahead, through a grove of Australian tree ferns, and continue left to the *John McLaren Rhododendron Dell,* named for the park's most beloved superintendent. Uncle John, as he was known during his 56 years as manager, lived and worked here from 1887 until his death in 1943. McLaren had a personal interest in rhododendrons, and he collected them—and many other plants and trees—from growers and breeders throughout the world. Over the years the *Rhododendron Dell* has expanded until it now covers 20 acres with over 500 hybrid varieties of the plant.

Born in Scotland, McLaren worked in the gardens of estates there and in the San Francisco Bay area before he was selected by William Hammond Hall to implement the park plans. A dedicated and hardworking man, he was concerned with the beauty of the park, and turned down many gifts of plants or shrubs that he felt would detract from its natural beauty. He was not fond of statues either, and for that reason many of those that stand in the park are almost invisible, hidden by lush bushes and trees.

Automobiles were another source of irritation for the park superintendent: The thousands of trees growing in *Golden Gate Park* needed fertilizer, so McLaren asked the city for the horse droppings swept from the streets. With the advent of the automobile, he had to find another source. (Aside from his expertise in manure, McLaren gained international fame in 1915 as the landscape architect of the *Panama-Pacific International Exposition.*)

The *California Academy of Science* can be reached by following the dirt paths through the *Rhododendron Dell* or by continuing along John F. Kennedy Drive to Hagiwara Tea Garden Drive and turning left. Three separate museums are housed in this building: the *Steinhart Aquarium,* the *Natural History Museum,* and the *Morrison Planetarium* (see *Museums* in THE CITY). All three are open daily; admission charge (phone: 415-221-5100). The *Jungle Café* on the lower level serves cafeteria-style meals and snacks.

Between the entrance to the *California Academy of Science* and the *de Young Museum* is the *Music Concourse,* another remnant of the 200-acre 1894 fair. Free outdoor concerts are performed in the ornate bandshell donated by Claus Spreckels at 1 PM on Sundays (weather permitting). A statue of Francis Scott Key, who wrote the words for "The Star Spangled Banner," stands watch at the opposite end of the concourse.

Across Hagiwara Tea Garden Drive is the *Pool of Enchantment* and the *de Young Museum,* the starting point of this walk.

Index

Index